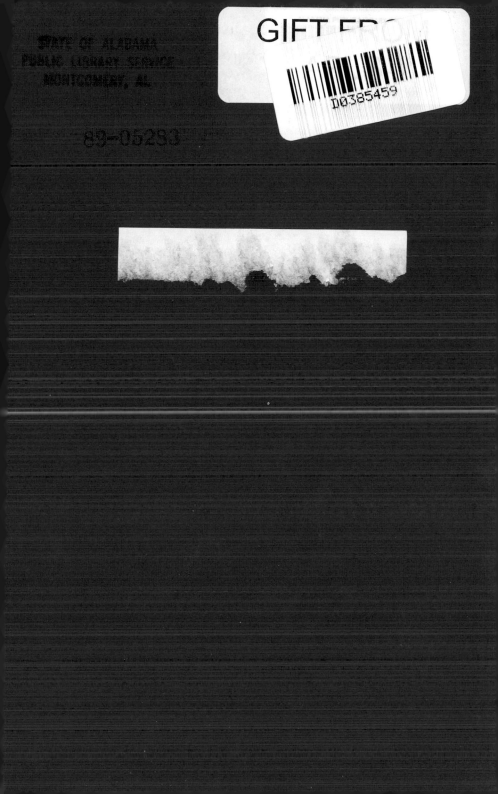

GREAT EXPRESSIONS

GREAT

EXPRESSIONS

HOW OUR FAVORITE WORDS AND PHRASES HAVE COME TO MEAN WHAT THEY MEAN

MARVIN VANONI

ILLUSTRATIONS BY CHRIS DEMAREST

WILLIAM MORROW
AND COMPANY, INC.
NEW YORK

Library of Congress Cataloging-in-Publication Data
Vanoni, Marvin.
Great expressions
1. English language—Etymology. 2. English
language—Terms and phrases. I. Title.
PE1574.V3   1989   422   88-31474
ISBN 0-688-07990-3

Printed in the United States of America

First Edition

1 2 3 4 5 6 7 8 9 10

BOOK DESIGN BY JAYE ZIMET

To my wife, Carol,
and to my son, Corbett

Special thanks to Teresa Chris and
Andy Ambraziejus for all their help

CONTENTS

INTRODUCTION

Researching the historical development of words and phrases, known as etymology, is truly fascinating. Every word has its own personality, ancestors, and story to tell. The farthest areas of the world have contributed to the English language. This collection of expressions was carefully selected to show the rich origins of our language.

Great Expressions will interest not only the general readers, students, and persons seeking to interpret English, but men and women of other linguistic backgrounds. This book is a genuine blend of information and entertainment. It is my hope that there is something in this book for everyone. In any case, may you have as much enjoyment reading *Great Expressions* as I had writing it.

—MARVIN VANONI

I

FARM AND COUNTRY

Chump □ **Curfew** □ **As the Crow Flies** □ **To Bawl Out** □ **Field** □ **To Go Haywire** □ **To Stump** □ **To Hightail It** □ **To Fly off the Handle** □ **Roughneck** □ **To Brood** □ **To Sow Wild Oats** □ **To Fork Over** □ **One-horse** □ **Tractor** □

Chump

Until less than two centuries ago, wood was the principal fuel used for both heating and cooking. There were no power tools, and clumsy saws of the Elizabethan Age were too heavy for one man. So the small farmer was forced to depend upon his ax.

It was common knowledge that a good, solid chopping block was almost as necessary as a sharp ax. Veteran woodcutters of Essex County insisted that the only satisfactory chopping log was a length of yew at least eight inches in diameter. In the vernacular of the region, such a block was called a chump. Gradually the use of the chump spread over the British Isles.

Since it was hard to conceive of anything more stolid, householders transferred the term to refer to stupid or dull-witted persons. Though new fuels seem on the way toward making the chopping block obsolete, the *chump* may never become extinct.

Curfew

The most fearful enemy of the medieval farmer was fire. His house was usually built at the edge of the forest, and if a fire broke out it would usually mean disaster.

In the winter, men working in the woods or fields had to keep a fire burning to keep warm. This was fine if they remembered to extinguish it, but of course some didn't, so a law was passed that made it mandatory to cover all open fires at dusk. Village church bells would toll the signal for *couvre-feu* (cover fire).

The British borrowed this custom and called it *curfew*. In time it came to mean the hour by which a person had to be home.

As the Crow Flies

This saying, which means the shortest distance between two points, came about simply because a crow supposedly flies straight to its destination.

In 1800, Robert Southey (1774–1843), an English poet, wrote in a letter: "About 15 miles, the crow's road."

To Bawl Out

Veteran handlers declare that the domestic bull is the meanest and most persistent animal on earth. When one of the big fellows becomes angry, he is mad at everybody and everything.

This was a routine aspect of early western ranching. Everybody knew that when a bull was rounded up, he was likely to bellow for hours. Such angry bawling was so commonplace among cattlemen that a man who berated another was compared to a bull and said to have *bawled out* the other.

Long a part of ranch talk, the term caught the public imagination in 1906. It was used by author/playwright Rex Beach in a popular novel titled *The Spoilers,* and its prevalence soared after that. The term soon swept the country as a way of describing a vigorous vocal display of anger.

Field

Our early ancestors could never have predicted our present-day shortage of timber. On the contrary, the British Isles were so heavily wooded that cleared land was quite scarce. After the Norman Conquest it became illegal to cut trees without permission, but before that period the young farmer's first task was that of clearing a plot of fertile land. Any place from which the trees had been cleared, or felled, the Anglo-Saxons called a *field*.

To Go Haywire

Moses P. Bliss launched a new era in agriculture when he patented a hay press in 1828. Prior to that time, the hay baler was simply a box with a compressible lid. Little pressure could be placed upon it, and loose bales were tied with string. There were many defects in the power press invented by Bliss, but others soon improved on his basic idea and began to make balers that pressed hay into firm bundles so that they might be tied with wire.

There was only one major difficulty: Stiff haywire easily became tangled. Frequently it got caught in the machinery. At other times it would wind about horses' legs or snag the clothing of workmen. Such accidents were so common that *to go haywire* came into general use whenever any device or plan got out of order.

To Stump

Though pioneers built their houses and barns out of logs, trees were so thick that they were regarded as a nuisance. It was hard enough to cut them down, but the stumps were an even more serious problem.

Frontiersmen frequently swapped work with one another in clearing new ground. After a log-rolling it was necessary to pull up as many stumps as possible. Some frontiersmen would brag about their ability to pull up the big ones, but it wasn't unusual for the boaster to suffer defeat with a stubborn stump. As a result, anything that proves too difficult for a person is said *to stump* him.

To Hightail It

During the days of the American West, many herds of wild horses roamed the plains. These beautiful animals were shrewd and very fast. It took a lot of skill to catch one, because at the slightest sign of danger the stallions would lead the herd to safety.

The men who matched wits against these animals noticed an odd trait. When startled, wild horses jerked their tails very high and then broke into a fast gallop. Consequently, cowboys spread stories about these untamed animals, and soon any person or vehicle that got off to a fast start was said to have *hightailed it* down the road.

To Fly off the Handle

Besides the frontiersman's rifle, his ax was probably the most treasured device he owned.

Machine-made ax handles were not yet invented; each woodsman whittled his own from oak, hickory, or gum. Crudely fitted to the stock, a poorly balanced ax was hard to use, and it wasn't uncommon for a pioneer to take a hard swing and have his ax fly right off the handle.

It's easy to picture the man becoming very angry at this. Fits of rage were so frequently associated with the loss of an ax that a person displaying sudden anger was said *to fly off the handle*.

Roughneck

Frontiersmen had no time for, nor did they really get too excited about, haircuts. Most would just gather their hair in a crude knot laced with a strip of rawhide. When it grew so long that it bothered them, they would cut it off with a hunting knife. It was common for pioneer men to have rough-cut hair hanging down their necks, and it became a practice to call these people roughnecks. A *roughneck* was usually loud and rowdy, so the name eventually came to mean a bully or tough guy, no matter how his hair looked.

To Brood

There is no evidence that early inhabitants of Britain kept poultry. Wild fowl were plentiful, however, and every child learned that mother birds have to sit on eggs in order to hatch their babies. Young birds "produced by warmth" were called *brod* from an Anglo-Saxon term for "heat." Eventually the term was modified to *brood*.

As householders began to keep poultry, it became a part of everyday life to see a hen brooding over her eggs day after day. People compared the stubborn fowl with humans who wished to hatch plots, and a person who persisted in keeping a plan warm for days or weeks was said *to brood*. Its meaning expanded by centuries of use, the ancient barnyard term eventually came to signify any prolonged act of pensiveness.

To Sow Wild Oats

Unlike wheat and barley, oats were once eaten whole. The Saxons planted the grain at least as early as the tenth century, and the Scots learned to beat it into meal a few generations later.

In the eleventh century, rural England was sucked into the whirlpool of war. Farms went untended while men followed their chieftains into battle against invaders from across the Channel. Land sometimes lay fallow for a full generation.

Under such conditions, many strains of oat reverted to their wild state. Young and inexperienced farmers, eager to extend their cultivated land, often gathered and planted wild oats. Such seed produced thick and luxurious blades, but very light heads. After a man had gone to the trouble of making such a crop, he seldom found it worth his while to harvest it.

It was foolish and wasteful to sow such seed, but old folks found they couldn't tell a young fellow anything. If he wished to try a crop of wild oats, they might as well let him learn by experience. Evidently a good many actually did sow wild oats—for the expression came into figurative use to indicate the indulgence of young males in sexual promiscuity.

To Fork Over

Most of the rich farmland of Britain was once owned by great lords who held title until the rise of modern times. Though money was scarce, it was customary to charge rent in terms of silver. Agents such as the notorious Captain Boycott (1832–1897) were merciless in their abuse of tenants. It was not unusual for these landlords to drive a wagon into a field as wheat was being cut. If the farmer could not produce enough silver to pay his rent, he would be forced to settle in grain—at a price well below the market.

Many a tenant gritted his teeth when commanded to grab a pitchfork and "fork over" the choicest produce of his fields, but he had no recourse. Captain Boycott refused to reduce rents and attempted to evict any tenant who could not pay in full. As a result, he was completely ostracized, his servants departed, and attempts were made to cut off his food supply. By harvest time, public opinion was so much in his disfavor that he had to import several hundred British soldiers to protect the harvesters—who themselves had been brought in from Northern Ireland. The Irish Land League, an organization of tenants, finally made life so miserable that Captain Boycott fled to England in 1880, thereby making the first boycott successful.

Spreading from literal application on the farm, the term *to fork over* came to stand for any enforced surrender of goods or money.

One-horse

Horses once outnumbered humans in the United States. As late as the turn of the present century, rural areas frequently averaged a dozen or more nags to a family. Many were used for plowing and pulling farm apparatus, but a man of any position also owned a pair of dashing buggy horses and enough saddle horses for each member of the family to have his own. Range land was plentiful, and it cost little to keep the animals.

So the man who had only one horse was operating on a very small scale indeed. His more prosperous neighbors tended to be a bit contemptuous of such a fellow, and any enterprise with limited resources came to be termed a *one-horse* affair.

Tractor

Late in the nineteenth century, Elisha Perkins created a sensation in the medical world. A pointed rod developed by the American physician was thought to relieve rheumatic pains when drawn over the skin of the sufferer. From a medieval Latin term for "to draw," his device was called a tractor—in the same sense as when an injured limb is put in traction, or drawn back into place. So highly regarded was Dr. Perkins's device that a pair of his tractors sold for twenty-five dollars in London in 1902.

Inventors and machinists adapted the same Latin root in naming the steam traction engine that came into use for drawing artillery wagons as early as 1830. Various kinds of such pulling machines were employed by farmers in both England and America.

In 1903 the Hart-Parr Company of Charles City, Iowa, developed a gasoline-fired traction machine with more versatility than earlier ones. Production ceased after fifteen of them were built, but company salesmen clipped the name of the traction machine to *tractor,* and it stuck in speech. However widely it departs from cumbersome early models, the modern tractor by its name perpetuates the idea of pulling and drawing, though the thing drawn is more likely to be a plow or a heavy trailer then a rheumatic ache.

EATING, DRINKING, AND GOING TO POT

To Sell Like Hot Cakes □ **Take with a Grain of Salt** □ **To Eat One's Hat** □ **To Make No Bones** □ **The Fat Is in the Fire** □ **Pie** □ **Pot Shot** □ **Coconut** □ **Caboose** □ **Go to Pot** □ **Cocktail** □ **Cocktail Hour** □ **Coffee Break** □

To Sell Like Hot Cakes

Sometime during the pioneer era, cornmeal was put to a new use. When fried on a griddle in butter, it became a fluffy treat—a thin cake—that was delicious while still hot. Rugged frontiersmen liked their hot cakes fried in bear grease; town folks preferred pork lard. But everybody agreed they were terrific.

Hot cakes were soon in great demand in work camps, boardinghouses, and at benefit suppers. Cooks couldn't keep up with all the requests for them. They became so popular that by 1825 *to sell like hot cakes* became a standard phrase.

Take with a Grain of Salt

Salt was rare and costly in ancient times, and people thought it contained magical powers. In addition to using salt as a seasoning, they threw it over their shoulder for luck and sprinkled it on food suspected of containing poison.

It soon became customary to eat a questionable dish only with salt. This ancient superstition has disappeared, but has left its mark in our language. When we doubt the accuracy of a statement, we sometimes say, "I'll take that with a grain of salt!"

To Eat One's Hat

Many a man, having lost a bet, has attempted to devise some ingenious way to eat his hat. In such emergencies a knowledge of this etymology would be of great value, for the expression *to eat one's hat* once referred not to Panamas and Stetsons but to a culinary product.

Napier's Boke of Cookery, an early British cookbook (1838), gives these directions: "Hattes are made of eggs, veal, dates, saffron, salt, and so forth." Exactly what these were is not too clear, but a strong stomach was probably needed to eat them.

Even so, the early bragger who offered to eat a hatte had nothing as inedible as felt or straw in mind.

To Make No Bones

Elaborate menus were unknown to common folk in medieval Europe. Cooking vessels were rare and expensive, so all the vegetables were usually boiled in a single pot. Unless a housewife had a piece of meat large enough to roast, she usually tossed it in with her turnips, beans, cabbage, and carrots. It was inevitable that the pot of stew should contain at least the neck, wings, and feet from a fowl or two.

Often the pot boiled for hours. Bones separated and dispersed throughout the stew. A person had to eat with some degree of caution, removing bones all the while. As a result, by 1450 a person making objections of any sort was said to be "finding bones." This expression came into wide use and soon people needed an equally forceful way of illustrating the opposite attitude. The phrase that evolved describes a person who plunges boldly into an undertaking as one who *makes no bones* about it.

The Fat Is in the Fire

Modern cooking utensils have actually revolutionized the kitchen. Until recent times only a few basic processes were in use. Soup was boiled, bread was baked, and meat was roasted.

Great skill was required to prepare a good roast. Not only did the cook have to get the whole piece done without searing it; the fat that dropped from it had to be saved. Used like gravy, the fat was a great delicacy. It was caught in a shallow pan and had to be stirred frequently.

Occasionally someone would spill the fat into the fire. That was a disaster because then there was nothing to moisten the meat with. *The fat is in the fire* entered general speech in 1560 and was used to stand for any unexpected trouble. In 1562, English author John Heywood (1497–1580) implied in "A Dialogue Conteyning Proverbs and Epigrammes": "Than [then] farwell ryches, the fat is in the fyre."

Pie

Until the late eighteenth century, the bird now called magpie was termed simply "pie." Then, as now, such a bird was likely to be a habitual collector. It was not unusual to find a pie's nest filled with pebbles, bits of broken glass, string, chicken feathers, and so on.

At some unrecorded time, an inspired housewife thought of placing a crust around a small pot of stew. She used whatever ingredients were at hand—meat, fowl, or fish, plus a few vegetables and perhaps an egg or two. Her menfolk liked the odd conglomeration and, casting about for a name, compared it with a pie's nest, which was filled with a variety of odds and ends. So they called the new dish *pie*.

First used in writing around 1303, the word came to include many varieties of pie. No other language has a word that is even distantly related to the name of the most popular of English dishes.

Pot Shot

Medieval sportsmen had many rules to govern hunting. Even then there were seasons for different animals and birds, and restrictions to give the hunted a sporting chance. But sometimes a man who wished to fill only his pot would come along and ignore all laws and regulations. Since rules were thrown aside when shooting for the pot, any cheap attack came to be called a *pot shot*.

Coconut

Portuguese parents of the sixteenth century threatened their children with the bogeyman if they didn't behave. They called the bogeyman *coco,* from a Latin expression meaning "skull." No child had ever actually seen a *coco,* but they knew it had an ugly face.

The Portuguese traders who first arrived at the Pacific Islands found a variety of palm trees that bore a large brown nut about the same size as a man's head. They were shocked to see three black marks on the nut—two eyes and a mouth. It resembled a bogeyman so much that they called it *coconut.* The word was soon adopted by the English and is still with us today.

Caboose

Medieval Dutch seamen were very daring and adventurous. In order to take long voyages, they devised a special cookhouse to use onboard their ships. They called this kitchen a *cabuse,* a blend of two Dutch words—*kaban huis*—meaning "cabin house" or "ship's galley."

About the eighteenth century, Dutch settlers in America used the term to stand for any small cabin or hut. By 1860, train crews across America had adopted *caboose* into their speech as meaning the last, or trainman's, car on a freight train. Incidentally, *caboose* has never been used by British railroaders. To them a caboose is a brake van.

Go to Pot

English squires of the fourteenth and fifteenth centuries didn't just eat beef. They also consumed large quantities of mutton and pork.

It is estimated that upper-class persons of that time ate at least three times as much meat as the average American does now.

Most men of that era preferred their meat roasted. After the best pieces were cut off a joint, the bone was usually given to one of the servants. She would take it home, trim off the scraps, and make a pot of stew. This practice was so common that it was customary to use *go to pot* as a way of expressing deterioration.

Cocktail

This word was born during the American Revolution when a barmaid who served Colonial and allied French officers their evening drinks decided on an extra touch. She began to garnish the drinks with the tail feathers of chickens stolen from a British sympathizer. This delighted one of the Frenchmen so much that he shouted out "*Vive le coq's* tail!" The name stuck, and now means any drink into which fruit, flavoring, alcohol, feathers, or any other item is mixed.

Cocktail Hour

One afternoon in the 1800s, a man entered the establishment of Antoine Amedee Peychaud, a New Orleans druggist. The man wasn't feeling well, so the druggist decided the best prescription for him would be a shot of brandy and bitters. Peychaud had nothing to serve it in, so he used an egg cup in which he usually mixed prescriptions.

In French-speaking New Orleans, an egg cup of the type Peychaud used was called a *coquetier* (pronounced "kok-tyay"). The ill man soon felt better and spread the word to all his friends about the great-tasting drink. Soon cafés advertised the *coquetiers* with window signs and added them to their menu. Since the term, cocktail, was already popular from the American Revolution, *coquetier* blended into *cocktail,* and the ritual of the cocktail hour emerged.

Coffee Break

The coffee break didn't become a recognized part of the business scene until the early 1940s, but it has been going on a long time. The practice spread from Arabia, where coffee was discovered, westward through Turkey, and then to Europe and the British Isles.

In eighteenth-century England, merchants transacted much of their business in coffeehouses, and the same was true in Colonial America. Lloyd's of London had its beginning in a coffeehouse. The first home of the New York Stock Exchange was the Tontine Coffee House, located on Wall Street.

The coffee break is as popular today as ever. A poll taken shows that between 74 and 94 percent of workers in the United States and Canada recess to the coffeepot daily for five to fifteen minutes of rest and mild stimulation.

BEAUTY AND FASHION

Bigwig □ **Blue Jeans** □ **To Cotton Up** □ **To Let One's Hair Down** □ **Stuffed Shirt** □ **Outskirts** □ **Widow's Peak** □ **To High-hat** □ **Best Foot Forward** □ **Sweater** □ **Permanent Wave** □ **Goblin** □ **Compact** □ **Bangs** □

Bigwig

The term *bigwig* comes from the wigs worn by British lawyers and judges in the seventeenth and eighteenth centuries. A bigwig can be defined as either a person of importance or a person who thinks he is important. To some of the lawyers and judges, the bigger the wig, the more important the man was.

Blue Jeans

In the Middle Ages many noted European cities specialized in the manufacture of some particular kind of cloth. This was the case with Janua (modern Genoa), which produced a heavy type of twilled cotton. This fabric was called jene or jean, from the fact that it was made in Janua. In 1495 King Henry VIII bought 262 bolts of it for use in the royal establishment.

Jean became popular for use in making trousers, and the name of the fabric passed over to garments made from it. For many years they were manufactured from undyed jean; then someone made up a batch from cloth dyed dark blue. Such blue jeans were an instant success with workmen and outdoorsmen.

In 1850, an impoverished immigrant tailor named Levi Strauss arrived in San Francisco with nothing but a bolt of canvas, which he hoped to make into tents to sell in the gold-mining camps. The cloth turned out to be too lightweight for tents, so when a miner complained to him that he couldn't buy work pants that would last, Strauss used it to tailor a pair of trousers.

The first pair made such a hit that other miners were soon asking for similar garments, and Levi Strauss was in business.

To Cotton Up

Ancient ruins have yielded scraps of cotton estimated to be five thousand years old. Cotton was grown and spun in regions as far apart as Egypt and China, yet it remained comparatively rare and exotic. Europeans could never get enough of it. Some of the great explorers of the fifteenth and sixteenth centuries were partly motivated by hopes of finding new sources of the fiber.

Weavers of that era didn't consider a piece of cloth finished until it was carefully rubbed to produce a visible down or nap. This operation yielded quantities of fluff. Bits of it clung tightly to the hair and clothing of workers, who picked it off with difficulty. So when a person was unusually tenacious—as in the case of a swain clinging tightly to the lass of his choice—he was said *to cotton up* to the woman.

To Let One's Hair Down

Through the centuries people have tried all kinds of hair styles. During the Golden Age of France, women spent much of their time elaborately fashioning fancy hairdos. Only in the privacy of their own home did any of these ladies get to relax and let their hair down. So this saying came to mean any person, male or female, who relaxed and temporarily put their troubles aside.

Stuffed Shirt

Few articles of clothing have climbed to the heights of popularity once enjoyed by the shirtwaist. Largely handmade in frilly styles and often stiffly starched, and garment was a trademark of American womanhood for more than a generation. As late as 1911, hundreds of New York loft buildings were filled with girls making shirtwaists.

Having no mannequins, many merchants of the era made window displays of shirtwaists stuffed with tissue paper. Such a figure looked dashing behind plate glass—but was actually very flimsy. Comparing the inflated talk of American males with these flimsy representations, people branded any braggart a *stuffed shirt*.

Outskirts

Dramatic changes in English life resulted from the successful invasion of the island by Norman warriors in the eleventh century. Norman ladies turned up their noses at the simple Anglo-Saxon clothing and produced an elaborate outer garment which they called a skirt.

The conquered people, awed by the fancy gear, noticed that a fringe of houses clustered outside town walls was similar to a skirt surrounding a woman's feet. Soon it was customary to speak of a city's edge as its skirt. Naturally, one who wished to indicate a house or inn located at the extreme outer border of the community described it as being in the *outskirts*.

Widow's Peak

During the Middle Ages it was the custom, and sometimes the law, that particular garments be worn by people in various occupations. There was even a ironclad dictum that widows wear special clothing. One of the distinctive features of their outfit was the pointed hood, or peak. One glance and it was evident that the wearer was a widow.

Emancipation of women made special clothing for the widow obsolete, but the pointed hood had made an impression on our language. Any person whose hair grows to a point in the middle of the forehead is still said to have a *widow's peak*.

To High-hat

Many quick fortunes were made in the Gay Nineties. Men who had been poor all their lives frequently won riches from timber, iron, cattle, and railroads. Many of them left their old friends and tried new lives in high society. They bought brownstone mansions, racehorses, and boxes at the opera. Splendid in high silk hats and long tails, they all looked the part of polished gentlemen.

Most of these newly rich promptly forgot the old friends they had known in poverty. It wasn't unusual for a man in a high hat to deliberately snub a former partner. These incidents happened so frequently that a person assuming a superior air was said to high-hat those whom he snubbed.

Best Foot Forward

For several centuries, titled European males were greatly concerned about appearances. They wore elaborate ruffled sleeves, powdered wigs, black satin breeches, and full-length hose.

Men of this class took great pride in having handsome legs. Many a gilded gentleman went so far as to give preference to one of his legs as being more attractive than the other. In order to make the greatest possible sensation at parties and receptions, he would casually stand with his "best" foot in front—where it would attract many eyes.

By the sixteenth century, *to put one's best foot forward* had come to mean an attempt to make a good impression.

Sweater

Professional horsemen of the nineteenth century developed many special practices for training racers. Among them was the use of a heavy blanket designed to introduce free perspiration during a workout. Obviously, there was but one name for the garment— *sweater*.

Athletes and sportsmen later made a fad of working off excess pounds while wearing flannel underclothing. Naturally, these garments were also called sweaters. About 1940, the fashion industry started to produce wool sweaters. They wanted the garments to appear more casual for the film stars in sports cars who set the style.

Permanent Wave

Scientific archaeology has provided positive proof that crude cosmetics were used in the very earliest periods of civilization. In Ur of the Chaldees, the city from which Abraham came, queens and ladies of the court were acquainted with eye shadow at least five thousand years ago.

At least since that time hair care has been a perennial concern. No real advance over crude curling irons was made until 1879, when Marcel Grateau perfected a gadget by means of which he produced the Marcel wave. It won followers in both Europe and America and had no serious competitor for decades. Then in 1906, a German coiffeur living in London developed an expensive and often painful twelve-hour process by which he produced what he called *permanent waves*.

Human hairs grow at a rate of one half to one inch a month for a period seldom exceeding two years. Most individual hairs then drop out; a few remain in place but stop growing. Because of these factors, no person has precisely the same head of hair for any great length of time. Nevertheless, the name for long-lasting artificial waves won a place in speech and is now so firmly entrenched that most civilized women have to have a new permanent every few months.

Goblin

About the year 1435, there appeared in Paris a bright red fabric unlike anything seen before. The ladies loved this colorful cloth made by Gilles and Jehan Gobelin. It was so much more vivid in color than previous red material that it was rumored the Gobelin brothers had sold their souls to the devil in order to learn how to make the dye! People accused the craftsmen of sorcery and their name was used as an expression for an evil spirit. Through the years a letter was dropped from their name and *goblin* was formed.

Compact

Stone Age women probably used juices to stain their faces and enhance their charms. As recently as the 1890s, pratically all makeup was applied at home. But soon ladies were carrying powder, rouge, and a small mirror in their purse. It wasn't long before a manufacturer began mass production of a little box that had a mirror in its lid and places for rouge and powder. These new products were advertised as ''compact beauty cases for milady.'' Almost at once the ladies shortened the advertising phrase to just plain *compact*.

Bangs

The term we now use to describe a particular hairstyle once referred to the way a horse's tail looked!

Money problems in the middle of the nineteenth century hurt many of the rich sportsmen. Some sold their stables and horses. Others merely reduced their staff and kept only their best animals. The shorthanded stable crews couldn't groom horses as carefully as before. It had been customary to spend hours trimming a horse's tail; in the new age of austerity, grooms just cut the tail off square, or "banged it off."

Soon bangtail animals were winning horse races everywhere. Designers took note, and it wasn't long before fashionable women were displaying their hair in *bangs*.

IV

ROMANCE AND
WEDDING BELLS

X for a Kiss □ To Set One's Cap At □ Grass Widow □ To Tie the Knot □ Curtain Lecture □ To Date □ Left-handed Compliment □ To Nag □ Wedding □ Tied to Apron Strings □ Bridegroom □ Husband □ Wife □ Flame □ Honeymoon □

X for a Kiss

The custom of using X's at the end of letters to represent kisses grew out of medieval legal practices. In order to show good faith, the sign of St. Andrew was placed after the signature on important papers. This sign was the letter *X*.

Contracts were not considered legal until each signer included St. Andrew's cross after his name. Then he was required to kiss it to guarantee his obligation. Through the centuries this custom faded out, but people associated the letter *X* with a kiss and it is still being used this way today.

To Set One's Cap At

A woman wishing to win a certain man is likely to be accused of setting her cap at him. This phrase goes back to the era when France was a major power. She had a strong navy and large fleets of commercial vessels.

French sailors called the head of their ship its cap, from an adaption of the Latin word *caput* (head). When the steersman was ordered to head for a particular point, he set the cap of the ship toward the goal. Soon the old term for sailing toward a definite spot attached to any woman who actively sought to win the man of her choice, and vice versa.

Grass Widow

During the centuries of the British occupation of India, professional soldiers usually brought their wives and children along when ordered to the colony. However, most military establishments were in coastal areas, where the summer heat was unbearable. Officers who could afford to do so usually sent their wives to the hills for several months each summer.

To the person traveling from the city to one of these retreats, the lush carpet of grass was very noticeable. It was natural for a man who had dispatched his wife to the hills to say jokingly that he had "sent her to the grass." Since her absence was frequently of considerable duration, the missing spouse came to be called a *grass widow*.

To Tie the Knot

Early marriage customs originated the universally used expression *to tie the knot*. In many places, especially the East, an ecclesiastical dignitary performed the marriage ceremony quite simply. He would lay his hands on the bride and groom in blessing, then knot together their sleeves or two corners of their flowing robes. No vows were exchanged; the act of tying the knot symbolized the permanence of the union.

Even today, in certain parts of India, the priest or holy man ties together the garments of the bride and groom at the conclusion of the marriage ceremony.

Curtain Lecture

Every woman knows that a man would rather be scolded at any other time than when he is trying to go to sleep.

In America in the first half of the nineteenth century, it was customary to hang curtains around four-poster beds. Several couples frequently slept in one room, and the wife who had a grievance usually waited until the curtains were drawn about the bed to begin scolding her spouse.

Furniture styles have changed, but human nature has not.

The *curtain lecture*—minus the curtain—remains a familiar institution.

To Date

Farm boys of the last century had a hard time of it. They got up before dawn and usually worked in the fields till dark. Then they had to milk, chop wood, and finish other odd chores. A youth was lucky if he got any time off other than Sunday afternoons, Christmas, and the Fourth of July!

If a boy wanted to take a girl out he had to plan it long in advance. If he wished to pay attention to more than one girl, he had to ask each to meet him on a certain date.

This practice of making advance engagements led to calling any boy-girl meeting a *date*.

Left-handed Compliment

Medieval Germans placed every possible barrier between commoners and princes to discourage romance. If a man of blue blood married beneath his class, a special wedding ceremony took place. This rite was distinguished from the usual one by the fact that the groom gave the bride his left hand rather than his right. To the casual observer it appeared ordinary, but a left-handed marriage hardly deserved to be called a marriage. Neither the man's wife nor children could gain his rank or his property.

No wife felt quite satisfied with such status, and legal complications frequently ensued. After the sixteenth century, the left-handed wedding ceremony was seldom performed, but an insult that masquerades as praise is still called a *left-handed compliment*.

To Nag

European households of the early Middle Ages had a problem with pests. Rats infested every nook and corner. Squirrels even nested in the thatch roofs or upper rafters.

Between the rats and the squirrels, the noise of gnawing was very disturbing. The Germans developed the word *naggen,* an old Scandinavian term meaning "to gnaw," and applied it to any disturbance as nerve-racking as the gnawing of household pests.

Eventually a person who gnawed at another by constant fault-finding was said to *nag,* and the word soon lost its earlier meaning.

Wedding

It was customary for Anglo-Saxon parents to arrange the marriages of their children. When a suitable match was devised, the couple who were to be married went through a formal ceremony of betrothal. As a part of the proceedings, the bridegroom-to-be gave his pledge, or wed, that he would later marry the girl in question and no other. This early form of wedding only guaranteed that they would become man and wife.

With the decline of this custom of requiring formal betrothal, the only public promise, or wed, was made in the actual marriage ceremony. Naturally, people of that era began to speak of the rite as the *wedding.*

Tied to Apron Strings

In some respects, laws governing land rights are less complicated now than they were a few centuries ago. There were once many statutes concerning entailed real estate, provisional and limited tenure.

Among these were laws defining a husband's rights in property attached to the family of his wife. Frequently a man could not gain title to such property but could enjoy the use of it during the life of his mate. This was popularly called apron-string tenure.

Women had ways of reminding their husbands that apron-string tenure could be terminated by divorce. A man tied to his wife's apron strings was in no position to argue; hence, the expression came to stand for any abnormal submission to a wife or mother.

Bridegroom

Modern usage has the word *groom* mean a male servant or stableboy responsible for the care of horses. But in the past, any person who performed a menial task of any nature was termed a groom.

Early marriage ceremonies were often followed by a feast that sometimes lasted several days. In many parts of rural Europe the newly married man was expected to act as table waiter to his bride during the feast. Because he literally played the part of servant to the bride, it was natural that he should be called the bride's groom. Contracted in popular speech, the expression became *bridegroom*.

Husband

Home ownership by average persons is a modern development. Until the close of feudal times, the masses were held in serfdom. These peasants lived in rough cottages that belonged to their masters.

There were, however, a few yeomen who belonged to the freeholder class. This was a hereditary honor given for distinguished service in war, or for some other unusual exploit. A man winning or inheriting it was entitled to the privilege of owning a home and a few acres of land. He was termed a *husband*, from *hus* (house) and *bunda* (owner).

Since a husband occupied a social and economic position far above that of a serf, he was an attractive matrimonial catch. Ambitious mothers were eager for their girls to win husbands. But by the thirteenth century, the title had come to stand for any man joined to a woman in marriage, whether he was a home-owner or not.

Wife

Though by no means her only task, weaving (known as *wifan*) was the principal occupation of the Anglo-Saxon female. At that time the general term for humankind was *mann*. So in order to distinguish between the sexes, the female was known as a *wif-mann*, or "weaving-human."

In time it became customary for a man to speak of the female with whom he lived, and who did the weaving, as his *wif-mann*. Alterations in spelling over a period of centuries have produced the word *wife*.

Flame

Slang expressions are usually considered to be recent additions to speech, but this is not always the case. For more than three hundred years one's sweetheart has been called a *flame*.

This usage developed because French poets often needed a term to rhyme with *aime*, their word for "love." One of the few words that could be used in that fashion was *flamme*. Many sixteenth-century love poems included couplets, one line of which ended in *aime* and the other in *flamme*.

Sophisticates across the English Channel prided themselves on their ability to quote French verse. Constant association of *aime* with *flamme* led them to begin using the latter term to stand for the object of one's love. At least as early as 1650 friends refrained from calling the volunteer fire brigade when a young fellow became excited about a flame.

Honeymoon

Today we still promise to "take care of in sickness and in health." And the first and, perhaps, best test of our endurance in this process is the *honeymoon*.

Since the sixteenth century, the honeymoon recalls the first month of marriage. Happiest and sweetest during this time, newlyweds were said to change along with the next moon— roughly a month after the nuptials were over. After the mead and honey wine of the first month, society has collectively agreed, ''the honeymoon is over.''

V

FROM LITERARY LINGO TO SLOVENLY SLANG

Know Like a Book □ Blue Book □ Cliché □ Cock-and-Bull Story □ Anecdote □ Penknife □ Back Number □ To Publish □ Blacklist □ Pocketbook □ Tabloid ⑴ Bummer □ Ain't It the Truth □

Know Like a Book

Frontier communities had very few books. Only the Bible and Webster's Speller were circulated on a national basis. So the books that were available were used until they literally fell apart. Mothers taught their children his or her letters using one of the two or three books available in the village. At times it was necessary for the mothers to commit these books to memory. So when a housewife was familiar with a subject, she said she "knew it like a book." This usage entered our speech as an expression that means complete understanding.

Blue Book

Since the beginning of government by parliament, English lawmakers have taken pride in that institution. Clerks adopted special insignia to designate official records.

When printing came into vogue, it became customary to bind parliamentary documents in blue velvet. A lawyer who wished to consult the ultimate authority was likely to turn to his blue-bound volumes. The impact of these official publications was so great that any authoritative tome, no matter what its color, came to be called a *blue book*.

Cliché

Until the invention of modern machinery, the printing trade progressed slowly. As late as 1860 most type was set by hand.

At one stage in the manufacturing process, a workman had to

drop his die into molten lead that was just at the point of becoming hard. This action caused a characteristic little click, a sound French diesinkers called a *cliché*. The word soon came to stand for the piece of type produced by the click of the die. Then it came to mean a bar or line of type one column wide.

When a cliché consisted of some nicely turned phrase, the printer might save it for future use. But because it was so easy to insert into a piece of printing, it soon lost its freshness. For this reason the old printer's term came to stand for any set of well-worn words.

Cock-and-Bull Story

The invention of printing brought great changes, not only in the transmission of literature but also in its nature. Fables and folk tales, carefully memorized, made up the bulk of fiction until modern times.

These stories nearly always pointed out some moral and usually had barnyard animals for characters. Antics and wise sayings of the beasts amused children for many centuries. But as a literary form, the fable was filled with the fantastic and the incredible. No one in his right mind accepted a story about singing cocks and talking bulls as literally true.

So when anyone invented an elaborate falsehood that deceived none who heard it, the tale was likened to a fable and called a *cock-and-bull story*.

Anecdote

Modern persons like to whisper a bit of juicy gossip or a "good story" to their friends. But this isn't a twentieth-century invention. As long ago as the days of ancient Greece, matrons (and mates) counted the retailing of gossip as a favorite pastime.

Such confidential tidbits were termed *anekdotos*, from the

words *an* (not) and *ekdotos* (published). Though most good gossip now quickly finds its way into print, the *anecdote* remains eternally popular.

Penknife

Until recent times writing instruments were a constant source of annoyance. Even fine goose quill soon lost its shape and had to be trimmed. People were always in need of a sharp blade to trim their pens.

This was such a problem that by the fifteenth century craftsmen were actually making special knives with fine blades. Carried in a sheath, such a *penknife* was a handy tool to have. When steel pens were perfected, the knife lost its special use and its name transferred to any small blade carried in one's pocket.

Back Number

Until late in the nineteenth century, many United States periodicals were issued at irregular intervals. Publishers frequently gave more prominence to the number of an issue than to its date. Consequently, it was common to speak of a periodical as a *number*.

Printed material was scarce in small towns and on the frontier. In these areas back numbers of newspapers and magazines were greatly prized no matter how far out of date. Sophisticated visitors openly sneered at this attitude. As a result, any person holding old-fashioned ideas came to be called a *back number*.

To Publish

Officials of the Roman Empire used the term *publicare* to mean "making public," or announcing state decisions.

Passing through Old French, the ancient expression entered medieval English as *publish*. Only an occasional writer used the modern form, for the word was current in more than thirty spellings. It was applied to such activities as making public the contents of a will, announcing one's intention to marry, and spreading news by word of mouth.

The invention of printing provided a new method of announcing, or publishing, matters of public interest. Eventually the word transferred from distribution of printed copies to the process of printing itself. By the time of Columbus, *to publish* was generally applied to the printer's work alone.

Blacklist

As late as the eighteenth century, practically all volumes of any consequence were bound in calfskin. Some publishers experimented with dyes and succeeded in producing small quantities of maroon and black leather. However, natural calfskin was cheaper, so for generations black was reserved largely for official records.

Prominent in this category was the town clerk's tome, in which he recorded the names of thieves, debtors, gossips, and others who were convicted by local magistrates. When a person was listed in the local black book, both his reputation and credit suffered. So it became customary to refer to any record of questionable persons as a *blacklist*.

Pocketbook

The pocketbook was introduced about 1510 by the Italian publisher Aldus Manutius. Tiny enough to be carried in the pocket, it usually contained religious matter, mathematical tables, and other useful information. Later publishers included blank pages in the pocketbook so that merchants could jot down important records.

Late in the seventeenth century, bankers devised a new kind of money—printed forms promising a certain amount of gold to the bearer. Holders could not afford to thrust such valuable pieces of paper into a pouch or wallet. It was wiser to place them between the leaves of a pocketbook. This became so popular that a craftsman developed a new money holder, similar to the pocketbook but empty of leaves. Though the size and shape has changed, the name *pocketbook* still clings to it.

Tabloid

Nineteenth-century advances in medicine made the British a pill-conscious people. Sugar-coating had not been perfected, so most pills of the period were bitter as well as large.

Then the firm of Burroughs, Wellcome and Company had an inspiration. If medicinal tablets could be compressed, it would be easier to swallow them. Therefore, more people would buy them. After a number of experiments the manufacturers developed a method of making a small pill. Since it was the compressed form of a standard tablet, they adopted *tabloid* as the trademark of the new product.

Advertising made the product well known. Consequently, the term came to be applied to other condensed goods. By 1902 the *Westminster Gazette* was advertising a new venture in journalism —its intention "to give in tabloid form all the news printed in other journals."

Burroughs, Wellcome and Company took the matter to court, contending that *tabloid* could be used only to refer to their pills. They lost the suit in spite of the fact that they had invented the word. Passing out of popularity as a trade name for compressed medicinal tablets, the term became permanently attached to half-sized newspapers.

Bummer

In the original German, a *bummer* was a loafer—a bum. When we bum a ride or a cigarette, we are comparing ourselves to the vagabond or hobo.

During the 1960s, no longer meaning lazy or drunken, *bum* echoed a sense of newfound freedom. This is when it became fashionable to "do your own thing," or to "find yourself." That's why words of carefree or neutral shading came into our vocabulary: *ski bum, beach bum*. And with our further sociological development, we are no longer to label street people or the poor as bums, but when we are in trouble we say we got a "bum rap" or a "bum steer." And as transfigured in the seventies, the word came to refer to any unpleasant experience, especially one that is drug-induced.

Ain't It the Truth

The use of the word *ain't* began in England in 1703 and quickly found its way to America in the first decade of that century. Surprisingly, the word bore no social stigma at that time—it simply was used as a contraction of *am not*. But by 1830 the contraction had come to be used for *is not* and grammarians buckled.

Ain't it the truth came into American dialect in 1915. Acceptable only in banter, this expression has always been grammatically wrong, but at certain times has always felt unexcusably right.

VI

LANGUAGE OF THE SEA

To Barge In □ **To Chew the Fat** □ **To Ship** □ **In the Doghouse** □ **Round Robin** □ **To Pipe Down** □ **Bitter End** □ **To Be at Loose Ends** □ **First-rate** □ **Under the Weather** □ **All at Sea** □ **Hand over Fist** □ **To Know the Ropes** □ **Slush Fund** □ **To Make Both Ends Meet** □ **Between the Devil and the Deep Blue Sea** □

To Barge In

Europeans who participated in the medieval Crusades were greatly influenced by their experiences in Africa. They brought home many novel devices and more than a few exotic words. Seamen were especially impressed by a small sailing vessel that the Egyptians used on the Nile. They adopted its name, which they modified to *barge,* and applied it to similar ships built in Britain.

Designed to sail in shallow water, the barge proved useful in canals as well as rivers. Eventually sails were abandoned and bottoms were made flat. Pulled by conventional vessels or by animals on the bank, the barge was sturdy but clumsy. Accidents were frequent, for once a barge got under way, it was difficult to stop it or deflect its course. By 1800 shippers were comparing hasty action of any sort with the heavy rushing of a cargo boat, and a person bursting into a situation was said *to barge in.*

To Chew the Fat

A few generations ago, seamen did not have canned or refrigerated foods. These sailors were forced to rely on a few foods that would not spoil. One favorite was salt pork. No part of the meat went to waste; even pieces of the skin were saved. If supplies ever got low, a bit of skin might be handed out to each member of the crew. It was tough, but the layer of fat on it was better than nothing. While attempting to chew a piece of this fat, sailors would sit around mumbling to each other, probably about their terrible food.

About 1870, *to chew the fat* was being used in print to mean any indulgence in idle talk or tall tales.

To Ship

Until the locomotive came along, there were no land vehicles able to haul heavy goods at low cost. Seamen, on the other hand, were handling bulky freight long before the beginning of the Christian era. Transportation was dominated by ships for so long that our vocabulary was permanently affected. We still *ship* goods— whether sent by ship, train, truck, or plane.

In the Doghouse

Husbands who are in the doghouse may not know it, but this expression goes back to the days of the African slave trade.

Profits in this evil business were great, but so was the danger. The slave trader was constantly worried about the possibility that savages would break their chains and kill their captors. Many of the Yankee sailors slept on deck, closing and locking the hatches at night.

Some sort of shelter was needed, so many of the sailors covered the poop deck with tiny sleeping cubicles. The small size suggested the name *doghouse*. Even the officers frequently had to sleep in them. They were so uncomfortable that *in the doghouse* soon assumed its present meaning.

Round Robin

Since the seventeenth century it has been customary to maintain strict discipline on ships. However, it was carried to such an extreme during the era when Europe was expanding her overseas colonies that it was dangerous for a seaman to register a legitimate complaint.

French sailors devised a method of escaping punishment for

complaints. They would prepare a written statement and every man would sign it. In order that no man should head the list, they signed in a circle. When the captain received a *ruban rond* (round ribbon), he couldn't tell who signed it first.

British seamen borrowed the custom and called it round ruban. Soon the term was corrupted to *round robin,* never remotely connected with the bird.

To Pipe Down

To transmit orders on big sailing ships, an elaborate system of signals was devised. A special pipe was used by the boatswain that would sound notes that could be heard even in a storm.

One distinctive signal was used to send all the men below upon completion of a task or termination of an assembly. At times a harsh captain would break off in the middle of a discussion and order, "Pipe down." Failure to obey would be interpreted as mutiny, so the sailors had to be quiet at this signal.

Cadets at the United States Naval Academy adopted and modified the expression. About 1890 upperclassmen would silence a plebe by commanding, "Pipe down!" Popularized by the midshipmen, the expression entered common speech.

Bitter End

Early English ships were equipped with a device called a bitt. It was a heavy length of log mounted on an axle. A cable was rolled around it, one end nailed to the bitt and the other tied to the anchor.

This cable, or bitter, was very important. If anything happened to it, there was no way to keep the vessel from drifting with the tide. So it was made long and strong. Occasionally, however, it proved too short and the anchor would not catch. This situation was very alarming. It occurred often enough to brand *bitter end* into speech, meaning any unpleasant final result.

To Be at Loose Ends

During the days of sailing ships, rigging the sails was very difficult. There were hundreds of ropes hanging about. If these were left free to ravel, a tangled mess would result. So every ship's captain prided himself on the good condition of his "ends"—the taped ends of his ropes.

When other work was slack, idle members of the crew became nervous and rattled. Many a captain was accused of ordering his men to keep busy by repairing loose ends.

In 1546, author John Heywood wrote of "some loose or od ende" in life.

First-rate

During the heyday of her naval expansion, Britain set up a classification system. Every warship she owned was inspected and given a category, or rate, which was determined by the number and weight of the guns mounted.

There were six rates, and seamen measured their own power by the rate of their ship. It was an ambition of every officer to be able to command a vessel of the first-rate. Standing as it did for the mightiest ship afloat, first-rate came to mean anything high in quality, on land or sea.

Under the Weather

This saying comes from the early seaman's language. When the weather at sea starts to get rough, tossing the ship about, most people go below to their cabins to try not to get sick. Those who went below were literally going *under the weather*. Soon the phrase was being used on both land and sea.

All at Sea

Early mariners frequently found themselves lost at sea. They had crude compasses as early as the thirteenth century, but these were clumsy and inaccurate.

Small ships made a practice of staying within sight of land. Sometimes, however, they were blown off course or dared to sail far out to sea. If the captain lost his bearings, the ship was in trouble. With nothing but water visible, the crew was literally *all at sea*. Borrowed from navigators, the expression came into general use to indicate confusion or bewilderment.

Hand over Fist

After the fifteenth century, sailing ships were equipped with rope ladders. These made it easy for seamen to climb into the rigging to trim or raise the sails.

When a gale blew up quickly, a captain might order most of his crew aloft at once. After having furled all the canvas, the sailors wanted to return to the deck as quickly as possible. The rope ladders were slow, so most men grabbed a rope and climbed down hand over hand. Speed of this descent led to the use of *hand over hand* to indicate rapid progress. By the eighteenth century the phrase had been modified to the more vigorous *hand over fist*.

To Know the Ropes

During the Elizabethan Age insufficient numbers of volunteers for the Royal Navy was a problem, until a practice came into use to remedy the situation. Rogues, vagabonds, and disorderly servingmen could be arrested and forced to work as seamen.

Such involuntary seamen were useless until they gained several months' experience. They were really helpless in the face of a complex system of ropes—hundreds of them—on full-rigged ships. It took some time before they *knew the ropes*. From the sea, the phrase came to mean any skill or inside knowledge.

Slush Fund

With no refrigeration, sailing ships of the nineteenth century had problems with their food supply. Salt pork was about the only meat that would keep. Whether fried or boiled, it produced a huge amount of grease, which was kept in vats.

Although this waste fat, or slush, was used to grease the masts, it always piled up. Tradition was that the slush was to be sold in port and the money used to buy luxuries for the crew. This early *slush fund* gave its name to money set aside from an operating budget—sometimes used for corrupt practices.

To Make Both Ends Meet

Sixteenth- and seventeenth-century sailing ships were complex. The larger ships had many masts and an elaborate system of sails. Each canvas was raised and lowered separately, and the rigging involved hundreds of ropes. Some were permanently fixed. When such a rope broke, most preferred to replace it rather than attempt a repair job.

Ship owners were sometimes short on money and instructed their captains to pull broken rope ends together and splice them. A piece of rigging was stretched to the limit in order for both ends to meet. *To make both ends meet* left the sea and entered speech to mean living within one's income, however meager.

Between the Devil and the Deep Blue Sea

The origin of this expression seems to be nautical in nature. In this instance, the devil is not the evil demon spirit but the gunwale of a ship or boat. It is a heavy plank fastened to the side of a vessel and used as a support for guns. It was difficult of access and, once you were there, a dangerous place to be, but better than the deep blue sea.

VII

SPORTS AND GAMES

To Get the Upper Hand □ To Bark Up the Wrong Tree □ To Win Hands Down □ To Ring the Bell □ Kite □ To Draw the Line □ From Pillar to Post □ To Start the Ball Rolling □ Nick of Time □ Down My Alley □ First-string □ To Have Something on the Ball □ To Rile □ To Knuckle Down □

To Get the Upper Hand

Gamblers of fifteenth-century England developed a game of chance that employed nothing more than a stick. The name of this game isn't clear, but the rules are simple. The stick was thrown from one man to another, then caught and held tightly. The first man would then press a hand around the stick just above the point at which it was being held; alternating handholds, they would move toward the top. Victory was achieved when a person got the upper hand—holding the stick leaving no room for his opponent to grasp it above his hand.

This practice is over five centuries old, but sandlot-baseball players still use it today with a bat in determining who will take the field in the first inning.

To Bark Up the Wrong Tree

The early settlers loved to hunt racoons and opossums. When these animals were pursued, they would usually take off through the thick underbrush. If a hunter's dog came close to a racoon, the racoon would climb the nearest tree. Barking and jumping underneath, the dog would keep the animal in the tree until the hunter arrived.

Sometimes, however, the racoon was smarter than the dog. After climbing the tree, he would sneak through the branches and hide in another tree. The dog was usually left jumping and barking under the empty tree.

From this, disappointed hunters coined a phrase to mean going after the wrong person: *barking up the wrong tree*.

To Win Hands Down

To win hands down means to win easily. This saying originated with horse racing. A jockey who sees that he is in the lead need not give his horse the whip, so he relaxes his hold on the reins by letting his hands drop. Keeping a firm grip on the reins explains the phrase *out of hand,* since a horse that doesn't feel authority of its master could go out of control.

To Ring the Bell

About 1890 strength-testing machines became a fad. Every fair, circus, and carnival had them. The machines were all different in some detail, but most came equipped with a bell.

When a person showed enough strength, a loud bell would ring. This would help attract other customers, and the bell ringer was awarded a prize. These devices became so popular that *to ring the bell* came to mean having success in any effort.

Kite

The kite was once Britain's most common bird of prey. Almost any day a person could look up and see one of these graceful birds gliding with the wind. The kite would spread its wings and drift overhead looking for a rodent to prey on.

About the beginning of the seventeenth century, English children learned to make a wooden frame which they stretched paper tightly across. When they pulled it with a string, it gained altitude and fluttered about much like the kite. So it was natural that it should be called a *kite.*

To Draw the Line

Tennis gets its name from *tenetz*, the English adaption of the original Arabic word *tanaz*, meaning "leap." Racquet probably comes from the Arabic *rahet*, meaning "palm of the hand."

Players used to strike a ball back and forth over a net with their hands. No equipment was needed except a net and a ball. Exact court dimensions had not been established. Players simply chose a level place for their net and stepped off an agreed distance in both directions. Then each drew a line which was the limit of the player's court. So common was this practice that by 1750 a person establishing a limit of any sort was said *to draw the line*.

From Pillar to Post

Tennis has been around for so long that its earliest forms have been lost in the mists of history. The modern outdoor sport of tennis is thought to have evolved from an indoor spectacle called *jeu de paume* (palm game), popular with French royalty in the fifteenth century.

In the early 1600s, tennis crossed the Channel and became popular in England, though few tennis courts were built because of lack of sufficient space within an estate's walls. Most gentlemen who took up the game played in their courtyards. Usually the front door of the castle would be one side of the court, the entrance gate in the surrounding wall on the other side. A quick game kept the players moving from the pillars of the mansion to the post of the gate.

Soon the phrase *from pillar to post* was being used as an expression to mean being driven from one difficulty to another.

It's interesting to note that the first book of rules for tennis wasn't written until 1873, by Major Wingfield of Nantclwyd in north Wales.

Also, the Americanization of tennis didn't begin until 1874, when a New Yorker, Mary Outerbridge, watched British soldiers playing the game at a garrison in Bermuda and returned to her home on Staten Island with two rackets and a couple of tennis balls. These were quickly expropriated by her brother, director of the Staten Island Cricket and Baseball Club, and put to use.

To Start the Ball Rolling

Croquet was not widely popular until it was brought to England by the Irish in 1852. Then it wasn't long before it was the chief game at garden parties and among weekend guests at country estates.

Croquet proved stubborn at one point, however. There was no way each player could have an equal chance. Given the first shot, an expert would usually reach the goal without a break. It was therefore a definite advantage to begin the game, or *to start the ball rolling*. This matter was so important that it caused the phrase to be applied to any type of beginning.

Nick of Time

Many years ago scores were kept track of on notched sticks of wood called tallies. In a sports contest the tally stick would be nicked each time somebody scored. When a team scored a last-minute point that brought victory to them, that nick was called the nick in time. The expression eventually changed to *nick of time*.

The wooden tallies, by the way, were a very important part of the official bookkeeping of the British government for many centuries. Records were made of sums loaned to the government and the tallies were notched as each payment was made. This practice was discontinued in 1826, and the lawmakers decided to use the old wooden tallies to stoke the fires in the stoves of the House of Lords.

Down My Alley

An alley was originally a walkway, but later the meaning came to include narrow passages, such as those between houses in a city.

When baseball became popular, *alley* came to stand for imaginary lines running between the outfields. A ball hit straight down the alley would usually mean extra bases.

Some baseball sluggers liked to brag that they had alleys belonging to them. When these sluggers got an easy hit, it was said to be *down their alley*. From the baseball field, this expression came to mean any task specifically suited to one's talents.

First-string

First-string and *second-string*, familiar sayings on the athletic field, originated when archery was the chief sport. Around the thirteenth century the longbow became a popular and feared weapon. Even most armor was no defense against it.

Men engaged in regular archery contests, and the best marksmen received a fine prize. In order to be a good marksman, an archer had to have a good bowstring. His favorite was naturally called his first-string. Firearms soon made the longbow a thing of the past, but first-string has stayed with us. The meaning has changed and is now associated with the best group of players on any field.

To Have Something on the Ball

In the history of sports, no other game has ever approached the quickness with which baseball rose to popularity. In June 1846, the first match game ever played took place in Hoboken, New Jersey.

Enthusiasts of the new sport discovered that the pitcher played a very important part. Soon, pitchers learned they could fool batters by spinning the ball. After throwing an effective curve, skillful pitchers were said by their admirers *to have something on the ball*.

The expression came to mean effectiveness in general. *Collier's* used the expression in 1912: "He's got nothing on the ball—nothing at all." The positive ran in *Mademoiselle* in 1935: "The lass has much on the ball."

To Rile

Some scholars think medieval French artisans used the term *ruiler* to describe the work of mixing mortar. From this, or a similar expression, anyone who stirred up mud in the bottom of a stream was said to roil the water.

Evidently some people were low-down skunks who deliberately roiled good fishing streams. As early as 1590, the term was used in figurative fashion. Even then it indicated the process of stirring up a person's anger. Nothing, but nothing, could make a sportsman madder than to find roiled water, which made it useless for him to throw in his hook.

Adventurers took the ancient term with them when they sailed to the New World. There they abbreviated it a trifle, and continued to use it both literally and figuratively. Hence, any process that annoys a person beyond endurance is said *to rile* him in the same fashion that a vandal can rile a stream by stirring up sediment from the bottom.

To Knuckle Down

Since ancient times, children have played games with little round balls. Long made chiefly of marble, the toys acquired the name of that stone.

About the sixteenth century, Dutch artisans discovered how to make marbles by baking balls of clay and porcelain. Given a new and cheaper source of supply, the game became popular with adults and youngsters. Late in the seventeenth century it looked as though marbles would become the national game of England.

The game was played in the following way. A standard ring or circle which measured about ten feet in diameter was drawn in the dirt. Thirteen marbles were placed in a cross in the center of the ring. The players took turns trying to shoot or knock the thirteen marbles out of the ring with a shooter marble. The player held the shooter marble between the thumb and index finger, and when he let go of the marble he was said to knuckle down. That meant that he had to keep at least one knuckle in contact with the ground until his shooter marble left his hand. The winner was the one who shot the most marbles from the ring. There were strict rules governing every phase of competition. One of the most important provided that a player should shoot from the precise spot where his marble last stopped.

George Washington, Thomas Jefferson, and John Adams were all avid collectors and players of marbles.

Spreading from the marble ring, *to knuckle down* became popular as a means of expressing earnest application to any task.

VIII

BUSINESS AND FINANCE

To Be on Tenterhooks

Prior to the establishment of laws protecting consumers, many manufacturers took advantage of a lax situation. Textile makers were particularly guilty. In early decades of machine-made cloth, it was customary to stretch fabric as wide as possible after milling. A cloth-stretching frame was called a tenter, from an early French term meaning "to stretch."

Rows of frames stood in the open air about many a pioneer factory. All the edges of each tenter were supplied with hooks. Wet cloth stretched upon tenterhooks might pull and strain and even split before shrinking. Since a person in an extremely uncomfortable situation resembles cloth stretched for drying, anyone caught in a dilemma is still said *to be on tenterhooks*.

Mad as a Hatter

Until just before the Industrial Revolution, masculine headgear was made almost exclusively of animal skins.

In order to increase the felting properties of hides used in making hats, mercury was extensively employed in the tanning process. Hatmakers, handling furs many hours a day over a period of years, gradually absorbed the poisonous metal. Consequently, many hatters began to suffer from the shakes in early middle age. A few years later mental disturbances would begin.

Soon it became proverbial to speak of any peculiar or unbalanced person as *mad as a hatter*. Popularized by Lewis Carroll, the expression entered the language—apparently to stay.

Brand

Not until comparatively recent times did it occur to anyone that hot iron could be used to make permanent marks. The custom of using such a heated tool arose with the medieval cattle trade. The glowing iron was called a brand, from an old Saxon term for "flaming stick," and the same name attached to the mark it made. Some smart manufacturer who wished to identify his wine barrels started burning his mark on them. By 1750 other packers who used wooden containers adopted this practice.

To Blow One's Horn

In medieval Europe, people made a constant display of their wealth and power. They not only rode in fine carriages and wore expensive clothing; they were constantly surrounded by a corps of guards and servants. When such a party rode into town, it was necessary to clear the narrow streets so they could pass. Heralds always led the group and blew their horns to announce the arrival of a person of importance.

Vendors and street salesmen also used horns to attract a crowd of patrons. Having no servants to do it for them, they were forced to blow their own horns. Their merchandise was hardly worth all the fanfare, so *to blow one's horn* came to stand for any sort of boastful or vulgar display.

To Shell Out

Money was scarce in Colonial America; not enough coins and bills were in circulation to meet the demands of commerce. As a result of this shortage, Indian corn was used as a medium of exchange.

All payments were in the form of shelled corn. Planters usually left it on the cob until time to meet an obligation. So when a bill was due, it was time to get the family together for a husking, or shelling out. This practice became so strongly attached to the idea of payment that a person handing over anything of value is said *to shell out.*

Down to Brass Tacks

Early dry-good stores sold piece goods by the yard, and merchants found it convenient to put tacks in the edge of the counter to indicate a yard, half-yard, and quarter-yard. Only brass tacks resisted rust and remained clearly visible.

The custom of putting price tags on merchandise did not become popular until the mid-1800s, so the housewife had to inquire about the price of an article. If she thought it too high, she would haggle in an attempt to get a reduction. After selecting several pieces of cloth a woman would argue until a price was reached.

All the haggling in the world made no sales. Only when the cloth actually went down on the corner alongside the brass tacks was any business transacted.

Dyed in the Wool

Some Technicolor movies set in the Middle Ages show the characters in a variety of brightly colored dresses and uniforms. Historical accuracy is usually lacking in such presentations, for modern chemical dyes date from the eighteenth century. In earlier periods even royalty wore comparatively drab clothing.

With few exceptions, dyes were of vegetable origin. They seldom retained their brilliance for more than a few weeks. This was especially true of woolen clothing, which was likely to be blotched and uneven the moment it was taken from the dye vat.

Then some artisan made a revolutionary discovery. Instead of dyeing finished garments or bolts of cloth, he dyed raw wool. Colors were much more firmly fixed, and fabric made of this dyed wool had a uniform appearance. As a result, it became customary to praise such goods as *dyed in the wool*. Eventually the phrase came to stand for high quality in general.

To Ring True

Metal workers of the late Middle Ages had very poor equipment with which to work. Consequently, coins produced at European mints were far from uniform in appearance. Matters were furthur complicated by a scarcity of precious metals, so that tokens, once in circulation, were worn smooth by frequent handling.

This situation gave criminals an opportunity that was too good to ignore. Great quantities of counterfeit coins were produced. Many were so crude that they could be identified by a glance. Others, however, looked as good as those which came from official sources.

When offered a doubtful piece, a tradesman would drop it on a stone slab. If counterfeit, it would produce a flat tone quite different from the ring of true coins because the metal used in its manufacture was of an inferior quality. This method of checking for quality was so common that any story or explanation tested and found acceptable was also said *to ring true*.

IX

ARTS AND ENTERTAINMENT

Dumbbell □ **Ringleader** □ **In the Groove** □ **To Come Out at the Little End of the Horn** □ **Discount** □ **To Play Second Fiddle** □ **To Pay the Piper** □ **What the Dickens** □ **On the Nose** □ **To Steal Thunder** □ **To Pan** □ **To Fill the Bill** □ **Behind the Scenes** □ **To Hop on the Bandwagon** □

Dumbbell

In the Middle Ages, bell ringing was considered an art. Bell ringers practiced for many hours and their noise often irritated the public.

Some unknown craftsman solved this problem by inventing a rope mechanism for beginning bell ringers. They went through all the same motions but pulled ''dumb bells''—different size weights—rather than real bells. This silent invention gave the apprentice bell ringer plenty of exercise. So when the early health fads started up, people called their exercise weights *dumbbells*.

Ringleader

The chief recreational pastime in medieval Europe was folk dancing. Usually the whole community showed up for the dances.

Most folk dances began with all the participants holding hands in a circle. At a signal the ring was broken, and one person or couple would lead the rest of the group in dance. It was very much an honor to be a ringleader.

Since this person was the mastermind of the dance, the title came to be applied to any person directing a group. Only in recent years has *ringleader* come to mean a leader in unlawful activities.

In the Groove

Thomas Edison's first talking machine, patented in 1877, was a scientific marvel, but it was a long way from being perfect.

Edison used a brass pipe into which spiral grooves were cut. Tinfoil wrapped over the brass was indented by sound impressions and reproduced them with some success. Things went well as long as the needle stayed in the groove. However, when it jumped out of place, the result was an uproar of noise.

A better machine with a wax cylinder was soon put on the market, and people were very much attracted to it. But every owner was cautioned to keep the needle *in the groove,* and in time the phrase meant displaying a good performance.

To Come Out at the Little End of the Horn

Medieval moneylenders frequently decorated their shops with representations of the cornucopia in order to attract victims. Usually shaped like a huge ram's horn, the cornucopia poured forth all sorts of good things.

Customers invariably got the worst of the bargain. Instead of the bounty promised by the horn of plenty, they usually gained empty pockets. It became a standing joke that a person getting the worst of it from a moneylender was "squeezed through the horn." A cartoonist of the seventeenth century even depicted a huge horn through which a young fellow was being pulled head first—minus his clothing. So much attention was attracted by this that any victim of a bad bargain was said *to come out at the little end of the horn.*

Discount

Tradesmen apparently began using the premium technique quite early. There is evidence that the Italians were first to knock off stated prices in bargaining. The French adopted the custom by 1500 and, influenced by Italian slang, called it *d'escompte* (taken from the count). Apparently, the practice consisted of selling merchandise by count, setting aside a portion of a lot when computing its cost.

Crossing the English Channel and emerging as *discount,* the premium in goods was abandoned in favor of reduction in price. As early as 1622, English merchants offered a discount on pepper sold in Holland. Its popularity spreading, the practice became so general that it became a standard device in modern selling.

To Play Second Fiddle

Early orchestras were made up largely of harpsichords, lutes, lyres, and flutes. But in 1624, Claudio Monteverdi began using various types of viols in harmony. By 1700, resources of the stringed instrument were well understood and first- and second-violin arrangements were adopted.

These instruments proved so effective that the device was carried over into popular music. Though the fiddle was a favorite instrument with common folk of England, few amateurs were content to play second parts. As a result, *to play second fiddle* came into wide use as a term for any subservient relationship.

To Pay the Piper

Street dancing was a chief form of amusement during medieval times. It was not every flute player who could pipe for a dance, however; so there developed a class of strolling musicians. They would play for a dance wherever they could gather a crowd.

Frequently a dance was organized on the spur of the moment. Persons who heard the notes of a piper would drop their work and join in the fun. When they tired of the frolic, they would pass the hat for the musician. It became proverbial that a dancer had better have his fun while he could; sooner or later he would have *to pay the piper.*

What the Dickens

This phrase has nothing to do with the famous English novelist. It is simply a euphemism for "What the Devil!" The expression was common centuries before Charles Dickens was ever born, having been used by William Shakespeare in *The Merry Wives of Windsor* (act 3, scene 2): "I cannot tell what the dickens his name is."

On the Nose

This phrase is a modern one, coming from live radio broadcasting. If a crew member at the station wanted to inform the person on the air that the timing of the program was on schedule, he would put a finger alongside his nose. Sign language is very common in radio and television because spoken instructions would go out over the air.

To Steal Thunder

For over two centuries we have used the expression *stealing thunder* to mean appropriation of any device or plan originated by someone else.

A little-known English dramatist by the name of John Dennis (1657–1734) coined the phrase. Dennis was educated at Harrow and at Caius College, Cambridge (B.A., 1679). In 1680 he was fined and lost his scholarship for "wounding with a sword" a fellow student. He never had a successful play, never married, and became poor and blind in his last years. John Dennis did have one bit of success: He invented a new and effective way of simulating thunder onstage. One of his plays folded and he discovered his thunder machine in use for a performance of *Macbeth* at the same theater. Dennis was furious. "See how the rascals use me!" he cried. "They will not let my play run; and yet they steal my thunder!"

To Pan

Miners in other parts of the world developed various ways of washing gold-bearing soil by hand. It remained for United States

prospectors, however, to reduce the use of mining pans to a science. Skillful movements could result in surprising efficiency in washing out dirt and impurities.

This process of sifting soon compared with critical evaluation of human performance. Just as the miner washed soil without finding any gold, the critic was sometimes hard put to discover merit in drama and literature. When nothing good could be said about a production, it was described as ''panned out''; the analyst was said *to pan* the effort.

To Fill the Bill

Prior to the Civil War, many theatrical companies were continually on tour. Advertising for shows was done largely through the medium of posters or bills. These were tacked up in a town several weeks before the first performance of a particular show. These bills frequently made extravagant claims. It took a proficient group of players to live up to the promises of the posters, or *to fill the bill*.

Comparisons between actors and their bills were so frequent that the theatrical term became a part of everyday speech.

Behind the Scenes

Development of the English theater proceeded rapidly during the long reign of Queen Elizabeth. More attention was given to scripts and actors than to stage settings, however. Most performances took place before a backdrop hardly more elaborate than simple curtains.

However, radical changes were made for private masques produced for the entertainment of James I and Charles I. Both of these rulers enjoyed the good things in life and encouraged free spending in the arts. Under their sponsorship, craftsmen began to create elaborate painted slides and hangings for the back and sides of the stage. Such pieces often represented a landscape in perspective, so were dubbed scenes.

In many plays and operas, important bits of action were reported rather than represented on the stage. This was especially the case with murders and executions, which were often treated as having taken place between acts. Patrons joked about the fact that such events occurred not on the stage but *behind the scenes*. Hence, real-life dramatic action hidden from the public came to be described by the term born in the theater.

To Hop on the Bandwagon

Phineas Taylor Barnum, America's first great showman, spent his early years in the mercantile business. At twenty-five he decided there must be an easier way to make money. So he bought a slave, Joyce Heth, who was reputed to have been George Washington's nurse. Any competent examiner could have shown she was not more than seventy. Undaunted, Barnum billed her as 160 years old, and in 1835 he launched an elaborate tour with her.

Joyce Heth soon died, so Barnum was forced to switch to such attractions as a clown, ventriloquist, and minstrel. He billed his show as "Barnum's Grand Scientific and Musical Theater." In order to attract a crowd he paraded through the streets of each town with his entire company perched on a wagon playing musical instruments.

Such a bandwagon had been used earlier, but it surged into prominence with the great showman. Political clubs built bandwagons of their own and gave rolling concerts in order to publicize their candidates. Small boys frequently climbed upon the bandwagon to ride with the musicians. Today any person who rushes to join a popular movement is still said *to hop on the bandwagon*.

X

WAR AND WEAPONS

Feather in One's Cap □ Pioneer □ Face the Music □ Bracelet □ To Be Unstrung □ To Get Hep/Hip □ To Egg One On □ Earshot □ Musket □ Flash in the Pan □

Feather in One's Cap

Women have laid claim to the use of feathers only in modern times. Sixteenth-century princes and noblemen went to great expense to import the finest feathers, which they used to decorate their hats.

Then someone came up with the idea of using small feathers as military decorations. If a soldier showed extreme gallantry, he was given a feather to wear in his cap as an honor. By the late sixteenth century this practice was so common that when a person won any kind of honor, he'd refer to it as a *feather in his cap*.

Pioneer

Specialization was developed among military units early on. There were fighting men on horseback and fighting men who walked. Cooks, paymasters, doctors, and surgeons accompanied Roman armies.

The Franks even had a special corps that went ahead of the army to prepare camp sites. A soldier didn't have to carry his luggage or level a spot upon which to pitch his tent. These chores were turned over to the *peonier*, who walked ahead of the troops carrying his spade and pickax.

By the sixteenth century the old army term was applied to any sort of advance labor. English modified the spelling to *pioneer*, and used it to stand for any person who prepares the way for others.

Face the Music

Until quite recent generations, most European armies were made up of professional soldiers. They took great pride in their corps and felt that life apart from it was hardly worth living.

But under certain conditions men were expelled from the service. If convicted of a crime that did not carry a death sentence, a soldier was imprisoned. After serving his time, he was brought before his assembled comrades and stripped of all military insignia. He was then ordered to leave and never return.

These ceremonies were carried out against the background of the doleful beating of a drum. From this early method of *facing the music* the expression came to be applied to any difficult ordeal.

Bracelet

Hand-to-hand combat made it necessary for the ancient Greek soldier to devise some kind of protection for his forearm, or brachium. Heavy leather bands were therefore created for this purpose. Ordinary fighting men wore plain bands, but the armbands of the officers were decorated with precious metals.

The Romans adopted the Greek armbands and later passed the idea on to Frankish warriors from the north. In their speech it was called *bracel* and became a standard piece of military gear. A woman who wore an ornament about her wrist was said to wear a *bracel-et* (little *bracel*). The invention of gunpowder made the armband obsolete, so its memory is preserved only in the decorative *bracelet* it named.

To Be Unstrung

If the entire history of mankind were taken into account, the bow would probably be found to be the most important weapon ever invented.

Despite its ancient lineage, this weapon did not reach its greatest development until modern times. English archers discovered that seasoned yew could be made into bows that stood as high as a man. An arrow from such a bow would penetrate an inch of oak at a hundred yards.

There was one difficulty with such a weapon. If kept under tension, the bow lost its resilience. When not in use, it was necessary to slip one end of the bowstring loose. This placed the owner at a disadvantage if encountered by the enemy.

It was a rare individual who could keep from quaking when caught *unstrung*. It is still used to indicate a state of nervousness or fear.

To Get Hep/Hip

Until modern times few military leaders concerned themselves with drilling their troops. Training was limited to instruction in the use of weapons, and there were no exercises compatible to the dress parade. Soldiers even straggled into battle with little system or order.

All that changed when troops were taught to march in step. Especially in centers where officers were trained, great emphasis was placed upon exact conformity to rhythm. Some time prior to the Civil War, drill sergeants at West Point adapted a new count. It had long been customary to mark each step with the right foot by shouting "Step! Step! Step!" Someone discovered that it was easier to say "Hep! Hep! Hep!"

In the early 1920s, jazz musicians began to call each other hep tomcats. *Hep* because they kept the proper beat (borrowed from the drillmaster's cadence), and *tomcats* because howling was their music.

The word *hip* is simply a variant of *hep*. By 1945, *hip* had replaced *hep* and, as one musician put it, "Hep wasn't hip anymore."

To Egg One On

Following the Norman Conquest, Anglo-Saxon peasants were treated brutally. Roped or chained together, they were driven from place to place like cattle. Many of the prisoners were urged to move faster by a poke by his captor's spearpoint, or *ecg*.

Later, children listened as their elders told of having been ecged on in this fashion. Tradition kept the stories alive long after

Anglo-Saxon ceased to be spoken, with the result that later generations referred to their ancestors as having been *egged on*. By this process the product of the hen won a permanent place in the language as a synonym for provoking or encouraging.

Earshot

Exact scales of distance have been developed only within the last few centuries. Land was once measured by shooting an arrow as far as possible. This didn't provide a standard unit, since the range of a bow varied from about 160 to 240 yards. But no other measurement was available, and as late as the eleventh century bowshot was an ordinary unit of distance.

Any point reached by an arrow was described as "within bowshot." So, any sound within range of the human ear was said to be "within earshot." Invention of exact measuring devices made the old unit obsolete, but anything that one can hear is still described as within *earshot*.

Musket

Various types of firearms were named after birds of prey. One of the birds of prey that were common in France in the sixteenth century was a small sparrow hawk called the musket. Though deadly on songbirds and small rodents, the musket was not nearly as fierce as the eagle or even the falcon. Since the musket was a small hawk, it was logical to give its name to a gun.

When we say small arms, we mean weapons basically designed to be carried by one person, as distinguished from heavy arms (artillery) developed in the late 1300s. The *musket* was developed in the early sixteenth century and was first used to shoot arrows. It was soon adapted to bullets and became the standard weapon used by infantry.

All early models were fired by means of a glowing wick, or

match, so two men were required—one to aim and the other to apply the fire. Clumsy and inaccurate though it was, the musket was the weapon that decided most battles for more than two centuries. Like the bird for which it was named, it was light enough for rapid maneuvering. Now of interest only as a museum piece, it was made obsolete by the invention of the rifle—which is actually a musket with spiral grooves in the barrel.

Flash in the Pan

American frontiersmen hunted game under conditions that would puzzle modern sportsmen. Their crude flintlock guns were a big handicap. When the trigger was snapped, friction between steel and flint might produce a spark, and it might not.

Even a strong spark did not guarantee that the gun would fire. It was equipped with a shallow pan in which a trail of powder led from the flint to the charge. Dampness or rough handling frequently broke the thin line of powder. In these cases there was a flash of light, but the gun didn't fire.

The phrase *flash in the pan* came to stand for any quick and dazzling failure.

XI

CRIME AND
PUNISHMENT

Clink □ **Falsehood** □ **To Seal One's Fate** □ **To Get a Break** □ **Caught Red-handed** □ **Side-kick** □ **In Cahoots** □ **Jailbird** □ **To Get One's Goat** □ **Stool Pigeon** □ **Head over Heels** □ **To Pull One's Leg** □ **Verdict** □ **To Throw the Book** □ **To Pull the Wool over One's Eyes** □ **Hue and Cry** □ **No Man's Land** □

Clink

Use of the word *clink* started around the year 1400 when English prison authorities in Southwark Prison began to use special iron chains. Prisoners constantly moving about with these chains attached to them made quite a racket. From the continuous clink of chains within the prison walls, Southwark was soon called "the clink." Gradually other prisons adopted these iron chains and used the term *clink*. Now any prison or jail is termed *the clink*—with or without chains echoing through its corridors.

Falsehood

Hats have come into use only in recent centuries. In the past, men wore hoods of cloth or fur attached to their cloaks. A man's hood would even give a hint of his occupation. Doctors, priests, and artists could be identified at a glance by the type of hood they wore.

This system had a few flaws. If a thief wished to set himself up as a doctor, he simply wore a doctor's hood and went to a town he was not known in. As a result of this practice, any deceit came to be labeled a *falsehood*.

To Seal One's Fate

Until a few generations ago, British law made death the penalty for many crimes. Every magistrate had the power to take the lives of the lawbreakers whom he judged.

In the late eighteenth century, many minor crimes were

removed from the death list, and the power of local justices was restricted. A death warrant was not even official unless it bore a proper seal from a high court.

A criminal had reason for hope as long as his death warrant remained unsealed. But after the official papers were signed and sealed, his fate was certain.

Soon *to seal one's fate* came to mean accepting a marriage proposal—or any other act that bound a person to a sure outcome.

To Get a Break

Beggars long ago discovered that they could increase their receipts by offering some sort of entertainment. It might be a juggling act, a crude show by a dancing bear, or some plaintive song. These and many other devices were used for attracting crowds.

At what he judged to be the right moment, the medieval entertainer would break his performance and collect the receipts. This practice was so common that in the speech of vagrants and criminals *break* came to mean "collection." By the nineteenth century, friends of a criminal sometimes made up a break to help him upon his discharge from prison.

No matter whether it was large or small, it was a piece of good luck *to get a break*. Picked up from the jargon of lawbreakers, the expression has come to be so widely used that it is now quite respectable.

Caught Red-handed

Criminal detection as a science was unknown before the middle of the nineteenth century. Earlier ages depended upon two methods: confession of a suspect by torture; and catching a man in the act of committing a crime. Circumstantial evidence was not admitted in court.

One common felony was the butchering of another man's sheep, pig, or cow; however, possession of the fresh meat wasn't enough proof of guilt. Only when a man was caught with the dead animal, with blood on his hands, could he be arrested with certainty of conviction.

So the expression came to be applied to surprising a person in any act of stealth, whether in violation of the law or not.

Sidekick

English pickpockets of a few centuries ago were very organized. Recruits went through apprenticeship, and a special vocabulary for their trade was developed.

They called a hip pocket a pratt and a breast pocket a pit. A vest pocket was known as a jerve, and a side breeches pocket was called a kick. No matter how nimble the pickpocket's fingers were, he usually had problems with the kick—since it lay so close to the victim's skin and was in constant motion.

If a man wanted to keep his wallet, he was wise to put it in his side kick. Later *sidekick* came to stand for a faithful partner who, like one's trouser pocket, is always at his side.

In Cahoots

In medieval Germany, large numbers of bandits lived in the regions surrounding the great Black Forest. Some had permanent houses, but the majority occupied tumbledown cabins. These were known as *kajuetes* and were shared by several men. Members of such a group were literally *in kajuete* with one another, so the term came to stand for any shady partnership.

Jailbird

For centuries, European law made certain crimes punishable by public display in a humiliating position. In England this was

usually an occasion for the stocks. But at times it was customary to place prisoners in large iron cages hanging a few feet off the ground. The criminal resembled a bird in a cage and they were soon dubbed *jailbirds*. The word caught the public's fancy and came to be applied to any imprisoned criminal.

To Get One's Goat

Racehorses are very high-strung animals. Trainers learned long ago that they enjoyed a stall mate, and goats were found to be soothing friends. But the use of these animals had its dangers. After a horse became fond of a goat, he would become very upset if separated from his friend.

Knowing this, gamblers used to steal a thoroughbred's stall mate a couple of days before a big race. This would upset the horse and reduce his chance of winning. From this practice, *to get one's goat* came to stand for making a person lose his temper.

The first appearance of the expression in print was in Christy Mathewson's *Pitching in a Pinch* (1912): "Then Lobert . . . stopped at third with a mocking smile which would have gotten the late Job's goat."

Stool Pigeon

As early as 1840, a spy in the pay of authorities was known as a *stool pigeon.*

Meat was highly prized by the British, especially that of the pigeon. They were a tempting delicacy. Birds brought down by gunfire were frequently damaged, so many hunters made their livelihood by trapping them.

The best method for luring a pigeon into a snare was by use of a decoy, or a tame bird. Trappers carried with them a small stool on which they sat while waiting for game. It was customary to tie the decoy pigeon to the stool so that it couldn't escape.

These "stool pigeons" lured their fellows into captivity, and the name came to be applied to criminals who betrayed their own class.

Head over Heels

During the Middle Ages, hundreds of crimes carried the death penalty. Two types of hangings were widely practiced: a man sentenced to execution was "hanged by the neck until dead"; and a man merely given a warning was sentenced to "hang by the heels." The expression *heels over head* came into use to indicate a state of helplessness or confusion.

Eventually the practice of hanging by the heels was stopped. People forgot the grim meaning of *heels over head* and changed the phrase to *head over heels*. Though it's meaningless in the modern form, we still use it to indicate helplessness.

To Pull One's Leg

Until fairly recent times, thieves operating in the back streets of a metropolis frequently worked in partnership with a specialist known as a "tripper-up." Using a walking stick with a curved handle or a piece of wire or rope, this person was highly skilled in the art of tripping pedestrians who wandered into the alleys. Once a victim was down, an accomplice stripped him of his valuables.

Since the robbers literally pulled the leg of a person in tripping him, the phrase entered speech to mean any mishap which leads to one's stumbling. Through the centuries it changed its meaning to making fun of a person, causing him to betray his ignorance. A victim of today's tripper-up is not likely to lose his wallet, but he may lose his temper.

Verdict

Trial by jury didn't come into prominence until the Middle Ages. It was believed that twelve was a holy number—since there were twelve tribes of Israel, twelve disciples of Jesus, and so on. According to medieval logic, twelve men in accord could not reach a false conclusion. In Old French, this body of twelve was given a technical name formed from *vrai* (true) and *dit* (said).

Though there is reason to doubt that supernatural power is ever used to find truth, even a modern jury cannot reach a verdict in a homicide case until all twelve members are in agreement.

To Throw the Book

During the 1920s most United States cities caught a wave of violence so severe that strong public sentiment was generated. Many states enacted strict laws aimed at habitual criminals; in several instances a fourth conviction carried automatic sentence of life in prison.

Many reform judges searched for the maximum penalty when given the opportunity to sentence an old offender. Underworld gossip warned thugs to stay out of such courts because these crusaders might "throw everything in the statute book" at the prisoner. The phrase *to throw the book* soon came to mean severe treatment by any authority.

To Pull the Wool over One's Eyes

A few hundred years ago, when all men of importance wore huge wigs, judges, being especially dignified, wore larger and longer wigs than anybody else. These were made of wool.

No matter how skillfully made, however, the wig was likely to be clumsy and at times slipped down over the eyes—making it hard to see.

Lawyers who were successful in tricking a judge would brag about having *pulled the wool over his eyes.* So the phrase came to stand for any kind of deception.

Hue and Cry

On the surface, the phrase *hue and cry* does not betray its use in early law-enforcement methods. But it came into being because medieval yeomen considered it great sport to hunt down criminals as though they were wild beasts.

Hunters of the period took their sport seriously and developed special cries to be used in pursuing various kinds of game. Consequently, by listening to the clamor of the chase, persons at a distance could tell whether the quarry was a deer, fox, boar, or other animal.

The legal system of the age gave accused persons few rights, so they frequently tried to escape rather than face trial. In such instances the sheriff and his men brought hounds and literally staged a manhunt. As they rode through the forest on the trail of the fugitive, they would give a distinctive hue and cry in order to arouse the whole countryside. Upon hearing it, every honest citizen was supposed to drop his work and join in the chase.

In later centuries the expression came to be applied to any loud disturbance, however innocent in nature.

No Man's Land

London became a major city more than a thousand years ago. Her twisting streets and crowded houses naturally were a refuge for criminals. Many of them were born in the ancient slums; others came there from the country. Methods of criminal detection were crude, but justice was severe. Death was often the penalty for minor crimes as well as major ones.

Authorities did not wish to clutter up the city with the bodies of those who were executed. So it became customary to take condemned men outside the north wall. There they were beheaded, impaled, or hanged. Frequently the bodies were left on display, as a grim warning to potential lawbreakers.

This went on for a period of many years. Cultivated fields and game preserves came to be established all around the places of execution. Titles were registered, and real estate came to be recognized as a major source of wealth. Still no one wished to claim the land where the executions were held. Long after the gallows was transferred to the city, the old death site lay waste. Since no one owned it, it was designated as *no man's land*.

From this early usage the term came to stand for any desolate or dangerous place. First used in a military sense about 1900, the old expression again became famous during World War I.

XII

FOR THE MALE

Stogy □ **Haymaker** □ **To Lock Horns** □ **To Keep a Stiff Upper Lip** □ **To Throw Down the Gauntlet** □ **To Court** □ **Not Up to Snuff** □ **Tobacco** □ **To Chew the Rag** □ **Better Half** □ **Whippersnapper** □ **To Henpeck** □ **Bald** □

Stogy

One of the first successful overland freight agencies in America consisted of a fleet of big Conestoga wagons that made regular trips between Pittsburgh, Pennsylvania, and Wheeling, West Virginia. Rough-and-tumble drivers, who liked their whiskey straight and their tobacco strong, complained that the slender cheroots then in vogue failed to give them satisfaction.

Accordingly, a Pennsylvania cigar maker devised a bigger, thicker smoke especially for the Conestoga drivers. Other men sampled them, liked them, and began referring to them as Conestogas. Shortened to *stogy,* the name spread to all types of cigars and won a permanent place in both the dictionary and the heart of the American male.

Haymaker

By the fifteenth century, any rural workman who gained a reputation with a scythe was likely to be called a haymaker. Since he repeated a few sets of motions over and over all day long, it was rather easy to mimic his actions. So there developed the haymaker's jig, a rural game or folk dance in which the workman's gestures were imitated.

Due to the influence of the dance, it later became customary to call a violent blow by a boxer a haymaker. Folk of good breeding never used the term, of course. It might have survived only among professional fighters had it not been for the rise of radio. Fight announcers in the 1920s dug up all the colorful old boxing expressions they could find and used them liberally in broadcasts. *Haymaker,* given new prominence in this fashion, came to stand for any blow good for a knockout—whether in the boxing ring or in a verbal bout around a conference table.

To Lock Horns

Various types of deer were familiar to early European hunters and sportsmen. They were a favorite quarry of kings and noblemen during England's age of chivalry.

Still, adventurers of later eras who left the island kingdom for New England were quite unprepared to see their first moose. Standing seven feet high at the withers, an old bull may boast antlers weighing as much as sixty pounds. He is a fearful, almost unbelievable sight.

Though males are shy and unapproachable during most of the year, they become aggressive during the mating season in autumn. Two big fellows sometimes stage a battle over a drab little cow, fighting savagely with horns and hooves. Nature offers few spectacles so grim as that of such giant swains with their spreading horns locked in battle.

Frontier speech was quickly enriched by comparing angry human opponents with battling moose. No matter how smooth their heads, persons who clash violently are said *to lock horns*.

To Keep a Stiff Upper Lip

Fashions in men's clothing are comparatively slow to change. But a man doesn't have to alter the cut of his coat; he has a fine source of variety in his use of facial hair. Men have been experimenting with it since the dawn of history. Razors were used in Britain at least as early as the sixth century, and for the past fourteen hundred years men of the island kingdom have alternately grown beards and shaved them off.

Clean shaving, adopted at intervals and then abandoned, first became universal during the age of Queen Anne. Men of the day

were scrupulous to cut off all their whiskers. Then, to make up for the loss, they donned clumsy wigs. When wigs began to go out of style, facial hair came back. Its advance was slow at first; military officers were the first to adopt the new style.

When a subaltern grew his first moustache, he sneered at timid civilians with their smooth faces. But there was one serious problem connected with the new adornment: It drew the eyes of all observers, and the least movement of one's upper lip made it twitch. That was a sign of emotion, and emotion was outlawed by the code of the era.

Stern old officers, themselves slow to adopt the newfangled moustache, roared loudly. If a young fellow insisted upon growing hair under his nose, he would have to learn *to keep a stiff upper lip*. Otherwise, the twitching of his moustache would indicate lack of emotional maturity and impair his standing as an officer and a gentleman. By 1833 the phrase had come to stand for self-control in general.

To Throw Down the Gauntlet

Knights of the age of chivalry were seldom as gallant and noble as they appear in the pages of romances. Many of them were actually rough, brawling fellows who divided their time between boasting, tippling, and fighting.

So long as opponents used only verbal abuse, there was no certainty that blows would be exchanged. But when a men meant business and really wanted to cross swords with a foe, he indicated it by throwing his metal-plated leather glove, or gauntlet, to the ground. This constituted his gage, or promise of battle.

There are indications that blustering was more common than mortal combat. Still, the custom made sufficient impact to affect general speech. By the time Drake sailed around the globe in the late sixteenth century, use of armored gloves had been abandoned. But *to throw down the gauntlet* still indicates any act of serious challenge.

To Court

Early in England's rise to power, her rulers began to speak of the royal headquarters as the court. This term was natural, for it was only slightly modified from the Latin *cohors* (enclosed yard).

Even kings have their ups and downs, however, and there were eras in which the court had only limited power. During the fifty-year struggles of the Wars of the Roses, central control was often very loose. Henry VII ascended the throne in 1485. First of the Tudor kings, he was determined to bring new dignity to royal business.

Under his leadership, England became unified internally. Then she began her commercial expansion that was to bring her into war with Spain. Careful, laborious, and systematic, the Tudor king reigned for a quarter of a century. He set up strict rules for conduct of business, and it became widely known that one who wished to advance in his favor must be fervent and constant. By the middle of the sixteenth century, any ambitious seeker for office or favors was said to "court" his sovereign.

From that usage it was an easy step to apply the kingly term to the most important of all diplomatic enterprises. For the past three centuries, a man paying amorous attention to a woman has been compared with a king's attendant and said *to court* his lady love.

Not Up to Snuff

Europeans of the seventeenth century developed a great passion for the use of finely powdered tobacco, or snuff. Englishmen of all sorts—rich and poor, learned and ignorant—were so inordinately fond of it that snuff was in nearly universal use throughout the island kingdom.

For some decades it was the custom for a person to grate his tobacco on the spot. Hence, snuff users were equipped with elaborate boxes that held coarse tobacco, with spoons and graters attached. Some were made from ivory and other exotic substances, while kings and emperors insisted upon having snuff boxes of solid gold set with jewels.

Use of individual snuff graters ceased with the advent of commercially ground mixtures. But connoisseurs continued to pride themselves on knowing their snuff. A sharp fellow, not easily deceived, was likely to be described as "up to snuff." Charles Dickens used this term several times.

It was natural that in popular speech a negative form of the descriptive phrase should be coined to label a simpleton or gullible fellow. At first the new label was used literally; one derided as *not up to snuff* was considered an amateur at judging powdered tobacco. But soon the phrase expanded to become a label of ridicule for any person or product considered to be less than discerning or below standard.

Tobacco

October 10, 1492, brought an end to the complaints of Columbus's weary and disgruntled crew members. For on that day deckhands fished from the waves a green branch with a blossom on it. Before evening they also found a reed and a staff that bore carvings clearly made by human hands. No doubt about it, they were close to land!

Soon the great explorer learned that he had touched a cluster of islands rather than the mainland of India, which he had been seeking. Still, as he proceeded leisurely from one island to another, he continued to send messengers—totally incapable of making themselves understood to the natives—to ask for directions to the palace of the Great Khan.

Strange animals, queer plants, and odd customs were encountered daily. True, there was no evidence of the huge gold nuggets that were supposed to be lying around in abundance. Neither did he find the spices that were a major inducement for the voyage. But other exotic things dulled the edge of his disappointment.

In his journal for November 6, Columbus recorded the report of a pair of men sent into the interior of an island on a scouting expedition:

"My messengers reported that after a march of about twelve miles they had discovered a village with about 1,000 inhabitants. The natives had received them ceremoniously, and had lodged them in the most beautiful houses. They encountered many men and women carrying some sort of cylinder in which sweetly smelling herbs were glowing. The people sucked the other end of the cylinder and, as it were, drank in the smoke. Natives said they called these cylinders tabacos."

Spanish adventurers confused the Carib word for the reed tubes with the dried leaves burned in bowls at the end of them, and *tobacco* entered world speech to designate the odd plant from the Americas.

To Chew the Rag

Another native habit picked up by Columbus's men was the widely prevalent custom of chewing the dried leaves of the tobacco plant.

Sailors sampled the weed, hesitantly at first, and then chewed with enthusiasm. Chewing tobacco caught on wherever it was introduced; within a century it was a national favorite in France, Portugal, Spain, and England. Soon the quid in cheek was almost as familiar a trademark of the sea as were tarred pigtails of the old salt. Landsmen took up smoking; sailors on wooden vessels were restricted to chewing.

Tobacco supplies were often exhausted on long voyages, and it was not unusual for sailors to turn to whatever substitutes they could find—meat rinds, soft leather, even rags. Rag-chewing sessions in the forecastle were so often linked with long-spun tales that any group of idlers who sit around talking are still said *to chew the rag*.

Better Half

Through the influence of the Puritans and other zealots, common speech was long pervaded by terms of a religious nature. Since the soul and body together were considered to make up man, one's more important, or spiritual, self was called the better half.

It took the genius of a great writer to see new meaning in the vivid expression. In his famous *Arcadia*, Sir Philip Sidney applied it to the union between husband and wife rather than that of body and soul. Although it was used to indicate either partner in the half-and-half match that is marriage, speech customs proved unable to stem the tide of male gallantry. For generations, therefore, every husband with a spark of honesty has used *better half* to name the woman who makes up more than half his life.

Whippersnapper

Lively young men of seventeenth-century England developed a great passion for fast driving. With two teams of horses hitched to heavy coaches, they dashed about in a style that made old-timers shake their heads and wonder what the world was coming to.

This newfangled sport required great skill in the use of the whip. No man was considered adept until he could flick a forward animal from below the lead bar without alarming the wheel horses. Oliver Cromwell excited great mirth when he had a crash in Hyde Park while driving four spirited animals recently given him by the Court of Oldenburg.

In this age of conspiracies, plots, and attempted rebellions, every swaggering bully prided himself on his prowess as a

whipsnapper. Naturally, adolescent youths and small boys tried to imitate their elders. Gangs of rowdies—boys who today would be called juvenile delinquents—made a great commotion by continually snapping and popping their long whips. This practice was so general that by 1700 any upstart youth or presumptuous person was likely to be sneeringly described as a *whippersnapper*.

To Henpeck

Part of the fame of biologist W. C. Allee rests on his study of what he called "the peck order among hens." Every barnyard flock, he said, establishes a definite pattern of social prestige. Any given hen pecks freely at those below her rank but submits to the pecking of those above her. Furthermore, the scientist has movies that show the peck order in operation.

Long before it came under scrutiny of a Ph.D., the hen's practice of using her beak as a weapon was noticed and made the subject of jokes. Aggressive wives were compared with fowls and said *to henpeck* their mates. Beginning late in the seventeenth century, novelists and poets began to poke fun at male submissiveness. Even Lord Byron joined the chorus. "Oh! ye lords of ladies intellectual," he quipped, " . . . have they not henpeck'd you all?"

Actually, such henpecking is practically limited to the human species. Ladies of the barnyard peck at one another with great fervor, but seldom use their beaks on a rooster. However, firmly established in the speech of millions who never actually watched an angry Rhode Island red hen pull feathers from a pert young Leghorn who just strutted past, the barnyard metaphor isn't likely to die merely because it is founded on fancy rather than fact.

Bald

All warm-blooded creatures have hair. Many are covered with it, while the whale has only a few whiskers and no fur coat. Humans are in a class all by themselves; most body hairs are very short, while the crop on the noggin is thick and fast-growing. That is, it is abundant on the heads of most females and some males. A minority of human males suffer from a condition seldom found anywhere else in the animal kingdom—loss of hair from the head. This condition is so widespread that hundreds of tongues and dialects include a special word to name the smooth-topped male.

Among the early Welsh the title was *bal* (white-browed). From this an early English hair-loser was described as "balled." In 1386 the great Chaucer wrote of a fellow who—said the poet—had a balled head that shone like any glass!

It was the whiteness and perhaps the glare in sunlight, not the roundness of a bare head, that gave birth to the title. For centuries any dog or horse with a white blaze on his head was likely to be called "Ball." Even now a distinctive white-capped bird is known as the bald coot. Regardless of the chain of speech that lay behind the term, Elizabethans liked to joke at the expense of the bald. They were likely to hail a fellow with a high forehead as "Old Peeled Garlic."

XIII

FOR THE FEMALE

Torn Between Two Fires □ Double-dyed □ To Raise Cain □ Pot Luck □ To Put the Bee On □ Gossip □ Formula □ Boudoir □ Hunk □ Alimony □

Torn Between Two Fires

The Normans who invaded England in the eleventh century took along many of their own customs and institutions. Among them were a variety of practices linked with knighthood and chivalry. Though crude and barbaric at first, chivalry was greatly refined during the centuries of the Crusades. Defense of churches, protection of the weak, courtesy, and gallantry were emphasized.

Eleanor of Aquitaine and other famous women came to symbolize purity and beauty. Any knight worthy of the name was expected to offer his life's blood in defense of the honor of some fair lady. Emphasized in this fashion, romantic love came to be compared with a blazing fire. Many stout swordsmen were proud to confess themselves all but consumed by "the fyre of luv."

Some fellows were unable to choose between sweethearts. Their hearts blazed not with one fire but with two. Under the circumstances, about all one could do was to pluck his lute and sigh at his misfortune at being *torn between two fires*. The expression, preserved in common speech for many centuries after the wane of chivalry as an institution, testifies to love's power in shaping language.

Double-dyed

Until the modern chemical industry made colorful dyes plentiful, housewives had many problems in trying to make gay clothing. They dyed their own homemade fabrics, often using juices squeezed from native herbs and berries. Color fixation was so poor that it became a common practice to dry material, then send it back through the vat. Such double-dyed cloth could be identified almost at a glance.

Lawyers and judges, searching for an expression to designate a hardened criminal, borrowed from the vocabulary of their wives. Consequently, any person deeply stained with guilt came to be called a *double-dyed* rogue or scoundrel.

To Raise Cain

No other volume compares with the King James Version of the Bible in its influence upon speech. Its impact was especially great in the late eighteenth century, when religious leaders turned to Scripture for rules to govern every area of life.

Most parents of the era were quite strict with their children. But occasionally a lax or indifferent father would let his youngsters run wild. Neighbors usually took it upon themselves to give a bit of advice in such cases. After making a pointed reference to the biblical story of the first murderer, the adviser would declare that Adam and Eve were largely responsible. After all, it was they who reared the boy who became his brother's killer. And the reasoning went that any careless parent was therefore likely to raise another Cain. Since the killer's name was synonymous with trouble and grief, any person who created a disturbance—by rearing an unruly child or violating convention—was said *to raise Cain*.

Pot Luck

Medieval gentry always had an abundance of rich food, frequently serving four or five kinds of meat as a meal. But families in the lower economic classes were constantly at the point of hunger. Often a struggle was required to get enough food to prevent actual starvation.

In order to stretch her food, a housewife would keep an iron pot on the open fire. She threw all her leftovers into it each day and kept it simmering much of the time. If a guest should arrive unexpectedly, he was likely to have to eat from the pot without any idea of what odds and ends had gone into it.

This early form of taking *pot luck* came to name the act of eating any meal for which the hostess had made no special preparation.

To Put the Bee On

Settlers along the Atlantic Coast of North America were delighted to find wild bees quite plentiful. When a family felt hungry for honey, the father or one of the older boys could almost always find a bee tree without much trouble. Frontiersmen noticed that the tiny insects always worked in groups and began to call any social gathering that combined work and pleasure a bee. Ladies had their spinning bees and quilting bees, men their husking bees, and entire communities had spelling bees.

Money was scarce on the frontier; so when churches were organized, the congregations were seldom able to give the preacher a cash salary. Instead they organized bees for him. All members of the community, whether they attended church or not, were solicited for gifts of work, clothing, or food commodities. This practice prevailed until the early nineteenth century.

Zealous collectors sponsoring a bee were not slow to put pressure on reluctant contributors. The result was that any person who made a determined request for a gift was said *to put the bee on* his victim. Later the term expanded to include persistent demands for loans and personal favors as well as gifts.

Gossip

Women are accused of being more prone to gossip than men. But the history of the word indicates that both sexes are about equally guilty.

Though the practice of talking about one another is probably as old as speech itself, Anglo-Saxon customs produced the modern expression. Saxons spoke of any relative as a sibb; hence, a sponsor in baptism was known as a godsibb of the infant. Slurred over in popular speech, the term became *gossip*.

Elaborate ceremonies of the times made it necessary for godparents, or gossips, to meet several times before and after a baptismal service. It was natural that such gatherings should be clearinghouses for community news. As a result, *gossip* came to be attached to all newsmongers and idle talkers.

Formula

Romans were famous for their precise, methodical ways. They performed most duties with great care and even wrote exact directions for religious and political ceremonies. Any pattern of words that was to be used without change they called *forma* (form). Short passages became *formula* (little form).

Centuries later, European scholars revived many long-lost expressions. Among them was the Latin designation for a form of words, such as a creed or an oath of allegiance. Every nation had its special formulas by which kings were invested with authority, soldiers addressed their superiors, and worshipers participated in religious rites.

Eventually the much-used term *formula* was applied to words used in a physician's list of medicines and a housewife's favorite recipe, which had to be followed as carefully as a formula for behavior at court. Spreading from such everyday use, the word gradually attached to unvarying sets of directions, such as those employed in chemistry, physics, and other exact sciences. Traces of the commonplace origin still cling to it, however; both the little recipe and the mixture produced by following the careful instructions for preparing a baby's bottle have the ancient title of *formula*.

Boudoir

In medieval France, no woman—regardless of her rank in society—had any legal rights. She was the liege subject of her husband and had no appeal from his dictates.

But even in the Dark Ages, women knew the value of tears. Having no other recourse, noblewomen offended by their husbands would retire to a cubbyhole and weep. The practice became so common that in wealthy homes a special room was reserved for this purpose.

Men loftily referred to such a room as the *bouder,* from a French term for sulking or pouting. When great ladies of England began to include private rooms in their homes, they appropriated the French term. Anglicized it became *boudoir*—whose literal meaning is ''the room in which the lady goes to pout.''

Hunk

Today *hunk* reminds one of narcissism, sexuality, and plenty of body work. This may have been amusing to the poor unskilled Hungarian immigrants who came to America around the turn of the century. Like mick or wop, hebe or kraut, hunk was not so much a description as an insulting remark. Because Hungarian immigrants often worked as manual laborers and their bodies were indeed built up, and because to say ''hunk'' sounded very much like a reference to a piece of meat (which these workers were sometimes treated like), *hunk* became a derogatory nickname for Hungarian men. Gradually the word expanded to include more than Hungarians—also Poles, Slavs, and Lithuanians. *Hunk* has finally evolved to describing just about any well-built male.

Alimony

This word comes from the Latin *alere,* which means "to nourish." The original sense was that of feeding, as in operating the alimentary canal. Many gentlemen languishing in alimony jail no doubt wish their ex-wives would study the derivation of the word and just ask for food. Even caviar and champagne would seem cheap. The word *alimony* in its present legal sense was used as long ago as 1655.

XIV

ANIMALS AND PETS

To Take the Bull by the Horns □ **No Spring Chicken** □ **To Browse** □ **To Ferret Out** □ **To Rook** □ **To Smell a Rat** □ **Chicken Feed** □ **To Talk Turkey** □ **To Be Fed Up** □ **To Get One's Back Up** □ **To Cry Wolf** □ **Eager Beaver** □

To Take the Bull by the Horns

Success of early ranchers in the American Southwest grew out of using a special kind of cattle and a particular type of man. It would be hard to say which of the two was tougher and meaner. Steers were rawboned and vicious; cowboys went out of their way to find thrills and danger.

Given such a combination, it was inevitable that men should challenge animals. Bulldogging, or barehanded wrestling with a running steer, became a standard sport of the range country. This operation is not for the timid and hesitant. There's only one way to begin, and that is by grabbing an animal's horns and trying to throw him. Consequently, popular speech insists that it is necessary *to take the bull by the horns* to start any action in which halfway measures can't be employed.

No Spring Chicken

No one knows just when and where men first kept poultry. Already an ancient practice by the time of Julius Caesar, this type of husbandry spread over the whole civilized world. Lacking incubators and warm houses, chicks couldn't be reared in cold weather. New England farmers of the last century found that those that broke the shell in early spring brought premium prices. So sharpers sometimes tried to deceive customers by offering old birds as though they belonged to the spring crop. Wise buyers would protest that a tough fowl was *no spring chicken;* hence the barnyard term came to name persons as well as birds that have passed beyond the plump and tender age.

To Browse

Grass-hungry animals of medieval Europe often resorted to nibbling on leaves and twigs of shrubs, even low trees. From an old term for "young shoot," the deer or ox that ate such stuff was said to browse.

Farmers who took their stock with them into the American frontier were sometimes hard pressed in winter. After hay was exhausted, cattle were turned out to browse. The nature of the coarse provender was such that a browsing animal seldom ate steadily at one spot. Instead there was sporadic nibbling and much moving about from place to place in search of something better.

It was probably an author, huffy over treatment of his books, who first compared halfhearted readers with cows moving from shrub to shrub. Once the vivid resemblance was seen, however, it quickly became proverbial. As a result, many a library that owns neither a cow nor a goat is equipped with a special room for use by patrons who like *to browse*.

To Ferret Out

Commerce between Europe and Africa flourished in classical times, then all but ceased for many generations. Consequently, plants and animals native to the dark continent were practically unknown to most Europeans as late as the tenth century.

Then traders began to bring over strange little creatures from Africa. Quite tame and trained to hunt rats, these animals were notoriously fond of eggs. So, perhaps from a corruption of the Latin for "thief with fur," the egg stealer was called the ferret.

Use of the pink-eyed hunter became widespread in the rat-infested cities of eastern Europe and Britain. The important animals proved adept in searching out burrowing creatures of all

types. It was both a serious pursuit and a popular sport to ferret for rabbits and other quarry. Charles Dickens picked up the animal-born term and applied it to detective work, with the result that a person who searches for hidden things, whether underground or not, is said *to ferret out* secrets.

To Rook

Noisy black birds of the crow family, living in large colonies, were long prominent in rural England. They preyed upon other birds and made life miserable for farmers by stealing seed, digging up tender young plants, and filling the air with their harsh shrieks.

Trying to reproduce the bird's characteristic cry, early writers called it the *hrooc*. Gradually modified, the name was applied both to the winged nuisance and to humans who behaved in similar fashion. By the time of Shakespeare, any petty cheat was compared with the thieving bird and said *to rook* those whom he defrauded.

To Smell a Rat

Civilized man has had few enemies so cunning and persistent as the common rat. Able to adapt itself to almost any climate and diet, this rodent has been a household nuisance since the Stone Age. Crowded cities of medieval Europe provided an especially fine haven, and rats multiplied until they outnumbered humans.

No house was free of the pests, so it was common practice to give terriers and other rat-hunting dogs free run of palaces as well as huts. In the course of a quiet evening, it was not unusual for the family dog to spring into sudden action. Whining, barking, and scratching at floor or wall, the animal would show all signs of excitement. If no more obvious cause could be found, the dog's behavior would be shrugged aside as caused by his having sniffed a rodent. This occurred so frequently that any person showing signs of suspicion was compared with the dog and said *to smell a rat.*

Chicken Feed

Pioneers who pushed westward from the Atlantic Coast of the North American continent took their domestic creatures with them. Chickens were high on the list of favorites, for flocks could live through the winter on grain too poor for use in the kitchen. "Chicken feed" became the standard label for stunted, weazened corn and inferior wheat. City slickers and riverboat gamblers borrowed the somewhat contemptuous name to apply to copper and silver coins. By the time Davy Crockett stories came into national vogue, it was natural to describe a confidence man as picking up *chicken feed* from the greenhorns whose small change he took.

To Talk Turkey

Spanish explorers in the New World discovered many strange plants, animals, and fowls. Among the latter was a huge bird that the Pueblo Indians had reared in domestication for centuries. It created a sensation when introduced in Europe about 1519. Few persons who saw it were aware of its real origin. It was so queer that people believed it must have come from Turkey—then a land symbolizing mystery. From the supposed land of origin the fowl came to be known as the turkey.

On the first Thanksgiving, which took place in mid-October 1621, four men were sent out to hunt wildfowl and brought back enough to last a week. There is no record of their bag, but it normally would have included the huge wild turkeys that were so plentiful.

English housewives regarded the turkey very highly; by the

end of the sixteenth century it was a common table bird on the island. Fowls raised there, however, never rivaled those which grew wild in North America. Settlers from England were amazed to find the forests thick with turkeys that might have weighed as much as fifty to sixty pounds. They soon learned that the gobblers were ardently polygamous. During mating season the big fellows chattered loudly and continuously, hoping to be answered by lovelorn hens.

Woodsmen discovered how to imitate the sounds of this fowl. After learning *to talk turkey* it was comparatively easy to maneuver a big fellow within shooting distance. Since it was a frontier joke that turkeys had no modesty and filled the air with their lovemaking, any person speaking frankly and bluntly was compared with a turkey caller.

To Be Fed Up

Few wild fowls have had so wide a range as the gray goose. Long ago it flourished from Lapland to Spain and Bulgaria and penetrated eastward as far as China. Charles Darwin and other observers noted that domestication took place very early. Except for an increase in size and the loss of brown feathers, bodily changes resulting from domestication have been insignificant across the centuries.

European goose farmers made use of nearly every part of the fowl—feathers, meat, fat (considered the best substitute for butter), and even the quills—long the most important of writing instruments.

It was found that by special feeding, enlargement of the liver could be produced—already highly prized for making pâté de foie gras, or goose-liver pie.

Goose fatteners, or crammers, operated chiefly in winter. Using fowls about nine months old, they placed them in cellars. Each goose was tied down firmly with plaited whipcord so that it could not move its body, legs, or wings. A typical cellar might include hundreds of fowls arranged in this fashion so that they could move only their necks.

Six times a day crammers used their middle finger to push into the throats of their geese a thick paste made of buckwheat flour, chestnut flour, and stewed maize. A man or woman who couldn't eat another bite of food compared himself with a stuffed goose. From this, literal application the term broadened so that a person who has had enough, regardless of whether food is involved, is said *to be fed up*.

To Get One's Back Up

Egypt may have been the region where small felines first formed an alliance with humans. Whether or not that was the case, early Egyptians had such reverence for the cat that they treated the animal as a demigod. The bodies of enormous numbers of cats were mummified in order that they might be preserved to enter the spirit world along with their human companions.

Until armies of Mohammed's followers invaded lands across the Mediterranean, the cat seems to have been unknown in Europe. Even when introduced, it made no great hit. But the multiplying hordes of rats in the centuries after the Crusades proved too much for familiar rat killers such as the ferret and the weasel, and the domestic cat rose to new importance.

No household was complete without a "hearth cat" (as distinguished from wild cats that still roamed in considerable numbers). In Germany, both Puss-in-Boots and Old Tom Growler became immortal figures in literature.

Through the centuries, however, cats have reserved a degree of their independence. They are more aloof and less docile than any other major domestic animal. No matter how well he has been trained, a sturdy tom will still scratch and spit when aroused.

Even for persons who have seen it many times, few sights are more interesting or impressive than that of an angry cat with its back arched very high, strutting about on its toes. This feline stance became so familiar to Europeans that as early as the 1500s an angry human was compared with a cat. Regardless of how great or how little change is made in the arch of the backbone, *to get one's back up* is used to name entrance into a state of rage, suspicion, or indignation.

To Cry Wolf

Chinese court life during the Chou Dynasty (1122 B.C. to 256 B.C.) reached a state of extravagance and corruption never equaled before or since. The slightest whim of court favorites was carried out, no matter what the consequences.

Emperor Yuan Wang (475 B.C. to 468 B.C.) fell passionately in love with Pao Si, a lady of the harem, because of her beauty. Many valuable pieces of silk were destroyed simply because Pao Si liked the sound of tearing silk. And in order to make her smile—after all attempts to do so had failed—the emperor thought of a ruse. He had all the beacons on the castle walls lighted as a signal for other feudal lords to come to his assistance against Western "barbarians" who were threatening the city. The ruse worked. The appearance of so many armed vassals, and their dumbfounded expressions when they found the call was a hoax, made the beautiful Pao Si rock with laughter.

The emperor, highly pleased with the success of his ruse, repeated it many times, until his subjects became bored and paid the war signals no heed. At last an enemy really appeared, the people ignored the alarm, and the city was captured.

Adapted into a plaintive ballad, the story was circulated far and wide. An unknown Greek used it as a model and wove the familiar tale of the shepherd boy who cried "Wolf" to make fun of villagers. From this adaptation of the account of the melancholy Oriental beauty came the phrase *to cry wolf*, still in wide use as an expression for spreading false alarms.

Eager Beaver

In the seventeenth and eighteenth centuries, beaver skins were fashionable, much as a Dior jacket might be today. The animal, which was especially desirable for men's high hats, was virtually unknown in Europe and had, in fact, been extinct on the British Isles for quite a while. Still, the animal was readily available in the American Northeast. Used as barter in New England in the 1600s, the beaver had a great deal to do with the forming of the Hudson Bay Company and the extension westward of the thirteen colonies into the wilderness.

The *eager beaver* comes down to us as a phrase coined by soldiers of the United States Army during World War II. They knew that the ones who volunteered too easily could be used for very dangerous missions. And in the American work force, an employee who is a little too enthusiastic and cheerful could easily become suspicious to fellow workers. In implication at least, like the beaver, he could be trapped.

XV

BUYING AND SELLING

To Calculate □ **False Front** □ **Wholesale and Retail** □ **Acid Test** □ **Hock Shop** □ **Budget** □ **Bankrupt** □ **Commission** □ **To Purchase** □ **To Let the Cat Out of the Bag** □

To Calculate

Many early Roman merchants built up enterprises that were quite large, even by modern standards. Their ships sailed all the known seas, and their great warehouses were filled with both staple goods and rare articles for the luxury trade.

No phase of their operations was more vexatious than the keeping of accounts. The cumbersome system of Roman numerals made addition difficult and multiplication all but impossible. Few businessmen attempted to keep anything resembling a ledger. Instead they kept up with shipments and receipts by arranging little rows of limestone pebbles, or *calculi*. Centuries of use only slightly modified the term, and it emerged into modern commerce as *to calculate*.

False Front

There have been many periods of booming prosperity, but none quite like the Gay Nineties. It was not only a period of quick wealth and free spending; it was also an era of complete optimism. Many persons thought such ills as depressions and wars would never return. In a wild outburst of enthusiasm, leaders blustered and bragged about unending prosperity.

It was inevitable that the mood of the era should be reflected in architecture. It became customary to build commercial establishments in such a fashion that the front wall extended well above the roof. This false front gave an appearance of greater size. Sometimes it extended a whole story above the roof and was equipped with windows that opened on empty space.

So prevalent was the *false front* that it came to be the symbol of pretense or any display of sham resources.

Wholesale and Retail

Defeat of the Spanish Armada in 1588 opened a new chapter in the history of the sea. It made no difference that the grand fleet of Philip II was battered at least as much by storms as by English cannon. What mattered was that England now had an opportunity to expand both as a major naval power and as a home base for ever-growing fleets of merchant ships.

As the size and number of vessels increased, owners altered their business operations. It had long been customary for a ship's master to parcel out her cargo to many buyers, but this became a nuisance as the volume of cargo grew. So more and more captains sailed under orders to empty their vessels as a result of a single transaction—to make a whole sale instead of a series of partial sales.

Used for several generations chiefly in a literal sense, *whole sale* operations came to be contrasted with *retail* ones. As a result, the sea-born term was attached to all ways of selling in gross—whether or not a whole cargo was involved. From commerce the term spilled over into common speech and literature, so that by the early eighteenth century Joseph Addison could be sure most folk would understand what he meant when he wrote about ''a wholesale dealer in Silks and Ribbons.''

By contrast, the retail merchant continues to count and deal in individual items—as indicated by *to tell,* the old word for counting that is kin to his name and that of the teller who counts money at the bank.

Acid Test

Now rapidly giving way to high-pressure salesmen, wandering peddlers were long a familiar part of the American scene. A typical member of the class carried a few household articles in a pack; if he was well established he drove a wagon.

Though he posed as a businessman, his real livelihood often came from buying old gold from his customers. Practice made it easy for him to separate brass from precious metal. But filled and plated pieces required a more accurate test than handling and examining. When in doubt there was a positive method for determining the value of a piece: the *acid test*. The buyer would file a shallow groove and touch it with nitric acid. Color reactions from the acid would show the approximate gold content. So frequent was the use of this method that any exacting trial came to be called by this term.

Hock Shop

Many expressions that were used by the Anglo-Saxons are so obscure that it is impossible to trace their development. Such is the case with their word *hock,* which may stem from a lost term for "lifting up"—as in the act of lifting a woman in a hearty embrace.

In the twelfth century, rural folk of Britain were enthusiastic in observing Hocktide. Falling during the second week after Easter Sunday, it was a season for rude festivities. On Monday, women of a community would lie in wait for men—then seized and bound them. No fellow was released until he made a small payment, which was turned over to the leaders of the parish. Men had their turn on Tuesday; that day they seized women and forced them to pay ransom, which usually took the form of a kiss, embrace, or small coin.

Any person trapped during Hocktide was in for some type of payment. Because of this it became customary to compare a captured villager with a person in trouble. Those who lost at cards, landed in jail, or accumulated debts were laughingly said to be in hock. The ancient term survived in slang expressions for many generations and erupted into new prominence when

twentieth-century Yankees applied *hock shop* to the pawnbroker's establishment. Unlike English villagers, most modern operators take their business so seriously, they wouldn't think of releasing their claims in return for a Hocktide kiss.

Budget

Struggling with a budget is no new problem; it dates back to the Roman Empire.

Latin housewives seldom had a regular amount given them by their husbands each week or month. Consequently, they were forced to be very cautious in their spending. This led to the practice of keeping money for household expenses in little leather bags, each holding a sum set aside for a specific item. This custom also prevailed among businessmen, who may have borrowed it from their wives—or vice versa.

Bulga, the Latin word for "bag," because attached to careful planning of one's finances. Adopted into French as *bougette,* it eventually entered English as *budget.*

Bankrupt

During the twelfth and thirteenth centuries, the republic of Venice was the commercial center of the world. Ships of every nation docked in her ports, and the Crusaders passed through on their way to and from the Holy Land. As a result, coins from all over the world circulated in her trading centers. This led to establishment of professional money changers, mostly long-bearded Lombards.

These gentry sat under awnings in the famous square of Saint Mark. Their stock in trade consisted of European and Near Eastern coins, arranged in stacks on a *banca* (bench) in front of them. (This is the origin of *bank.*) When a money changer was robbed of his capital or made insolvent by some other cause, it was customary for him to smash his bench.

Creditors were out of luck in such cases—a man was obviously in no shape to pay when he had a *banca rotta* (broken bench). Borrowed by English merchants as *bankrupt,* the term came to stand for insolvency in general.

Commission

At the height of her glory, imperial Rome dominated dozens of formerly independent kingdoms. Treaties and pacts were constantly being drawn up and sent to the far corners of the world for approval by some prince. The messenger carrying a royal document was said to bear a *commission,* from a term for "entrusted." Passing through Old French, the term became current in English about a century before the time of Columbus.

It long designated pay for services as an agent. Thus, a diplomatic messenger was listed on the payroll as a commissioner. Commission was usually on an agreed-salary basis and was paid to such diverse agents as tax collectors, sea captains, and wandering tradesmen. As late as the eighteenth century, Daniel Defoe, author of *Robinson Crusoe,* used *commission* in about the same sense we now use *wages.*

But the commercial world gradually adopted a faster pace. Merchants discovered that a sea captain was likely to be commissioner for half a dozen rivals as well as for his chief employer. Someone thought of offering the commissioner a percentage of profits rather than a flat fee. This type of inducement proved so effective that modern commission systems came into being.

To Purchase

Modern merchandising methods have developed within the past few generations. Formerly there was little or no systematic attempt to make consumer goods easily available to prospective buyers. Even in the late Middle Ages there were no stores at all, in the modern sense. Merchants occupied small booths or shops having neither show windows nor display counters. There were no newspapers in which to advertise. So the only means of acquainting the public with one's stock of goods was to station an apprentice at the door to recite a monotonous list of commodities on hand.

Consequently, a person desiring a particular article had to get out and hunt for it. Every successful shopping trip was a minor personal triumph. So many difficulties were involved that the process of searching became associated with the actual buying and produced the term *purchacier* (Old French, meaning "to chase" or "to seek ardently"). So many people chased so many bargains ardently that the label stuck in speech. Changes in spelling brought it into the modern form: *to purchase*.

To Let the Cat Out of the Bag

Not all lawbreakers are professional criminals. Given sufficient temptation and a good opportunity to get away with them, respectable middle-class citizens throughout history have been guilty of dishonest practices. By a curious set of circumstances, *to let the cat out of the bag* grew out of the activities of medieval swindlers. No professed thieves, these sharpers were "honest farmers."

When the Moslems invaded southern Europe early in the eighth century, one of the first edicts issued in conquered territory made it illegal to sell pork—for Mohammed had declared the pig unclean. Naturally, farmers in the hills hid their pigs and continued to enjoy sausage and ham. Pork-hungry city dwellers flocked to the country at every opportunity. They bought many suckling pigs, which were considered an especial delicacy and were easy to carry.

Bootleg transactions usually took place under cover of darkness, so farmers often tied up a cat in a sack and sold it as a young pig. A pork lover who opened such a container to gloat over his prize literally let the cat out of the bag. So common was this early type of dishonesty that the expression crept into polite speech to mean revealing any secret.

XVI

HOME AND GARDEN

Chair □ Threshold □ Weeds □ To Nip in the Bud □ Garden □ Mezzanine □ To Get Up on the Wrong Side of the Bed □ Window □ Furniture □ Bureau □

Chair

Pieces of furniture designed for use by a single person have come to be common and cheap only in modern times. During the Middle Ages, such a sitting piece was costly and relatively rare. In gatherings of all kinds, ordinary folk sat on the floor or upon benches. Only persons of importance had their own movable perches.

From the Greek *kathedra,* any four-legged piece of furniture with a back and two arms was known as a *cathedra* to Latin-speaking men of letters. Such a piece was used by a king on state occasions, by a judge presiding over court, by a mayor holding town council, and by a bishop exercising his office. Because the piece of furniture was the symbol of office and authority, to speak *ex cathedra* (from the chair) came to mean exercise of one's power to speak, expecting obedience with no questions asked.

As medieval universities multiplied after the thirteenth century, the piece of furniture signifying rank and dignity was naturally more and more common in places of learning. Students customarily occupied benches; only a professor could sit in a chair. So much sitting was done with so much pomp by so many learned doctors that most other roles of the chair dwindled in importance by comparison. A professorship is still known as a chair in spite of the fact that such a piece of furniture is supplied to each student in a modern classroom. Benefactors of colleges and universities often established an "endowed chair," and a professor is likely to refer to himself as "occupying the chair of English." Reflecting on this situation more than a century ago, Ralph Waldo Emerson needled the academic world by insisting that "many chairs are made beds of ease." No doubt he did mean professional chairs and not sitting pieces for students.

Threshold

Until modern farming methods began to produce a surplus, life actually depended on the annual harvest. Small grains were staple items in many cultures. Among the Anglo-Saxons, no ceremony was more important than *threscan,* during which men, women, and children eagerly trod on piles of dry wheat to separate grain from stalks.

Upon stepping into the entrance of a house, most persons halted to wipe their feet against the big block of wood or stone that marked the doorway. This operation bore more than a little resemblance to the shuffling of feet on the threshing floor. From this origin the sill where one repeats the foot movement reminiscent of the ancient harvest is still termed the *threshold* of a home.

Weeds

Men who practiced the first crude attempts to cultivate selected plants were annoyed by the intrusion of varieties they didn't want in their fields. From a variant of their term for "wild," early Saxons used *wiod* to name any obnoxious plant.

So old and important is the word that it is found in documents dating from the ninth century. The spelling was modified slightly, so that the earliest of English farm manuals agreed on stressing the necessity that *weeds* be kept under control.

Many varieties were given individual titles: cudweed, duckweed, dyer's weed, hogweed, ironweed, knotweed, milkweed, mugweed, and so on. In spite of the multiplicity of names for specific kinds of intruders, the ancient all-inclusive label clings in speech as a reminder that farmers must remain vigilant in their effort to protect cultivated plants from the encroachment of sturdy and aggressive wild ones.

To Nip in the Bud

Crude beginnings in scientific horticulture were made many centuries ago. At least as early as the fourteenth century, gardeners were aware that many plants produce an excessive number of blossoms. So it became customary to pinch off the majority in order for those that were left to produce large fruit.

This practice improved the quality of garden produce, but was more than a little severe upon individual buds. It became proverbial that when a bud was nipped off, no fruit would come from it. By the time of Shakespeare, the gardening practice was compared with human activities, and a person who calls an early halt to an enterprise or plan is said *to nip it in the bud*.

Garden

Their military fame has somewhat obscured the fact that early Romans were skillful growers of fruits and vegetables. Many estates boasted carefully worked gardens. From the name for garden, *hortus,* we get the term *horticulture*. Horticulturists who flourished under the Caesars actually launched gardening in Britain. They introduced the cherry to the island sometime during the first century and took the grapevine there during the third century.

Rome was forced to abandon her island outpost in the fifth century. Natives were little interested in growing kitchen foods, so gardening continued to flourish chiefly in connection with religious institutions.

Nearly every abbey and monastery had its own fruits, vegetables, and herbs. In order to protect precious rows of plants from wandering cattle, monks began to build walls and fences around cultivated plots. Popular speech of the period termed such a guarded place a *gardin*, which was modified to *garden*. The name of the cultivated spots so highly prized by medieval monks became attached to all small fields planted for household use, guarded or not.

Mezzanine

During the gilded centuries that marked the beginning of modern European history, architects had a field day. For their wealthy patrons they built ornate mansions that are still marvels of beauty—but considerably less than comfortable. One of the worst features of many palaces was the long stairway that had to be climbed between floors.

So one builder had an inspiration. Why not, said he, insert a partial middle story between the ground and second floors? It could be arranged as a row of rooms running about the midsection of towering ground-floor halls. Once tried, the innovation proved popular. It was logical to name it from *mezzanino* (middle). Some princely families found the *mezzanino* so comfortable that they reserved this level for their living quarters.

Slightly modified in passing through French into English, the sonorous Italian term for the extra floor in the middle became *mezzanine*. Precisely the same root furnished *mezzo-soprano* as a label for a singer whose voice lies between classical ranges.

To Get Up on the Wrong Side of the Bed

Few superstitions have been more widely held than those concerning the sinister nature of "the left." At least as early as the Roman Empire, a left-handed person was considered to be a bearer of bad luck. Any act involving the left was regarded with suspicion and dread.

This idea even affected common attitudes toward such objects as furniture. For example, a wise person made it a habit to get out of bed on the right side. If he occasionally crawled out on the left side, bad luck was almost certain to follow.

A person expected to encounter trouble is seldom in the best of moods. So irritability came to be associated with getting out of bed on the left, or wrong, side. This notion was so widely accepted that when we encounter an ill-natured person, we still accuse him of having *gotten up on the wrong side of the bed.*

Window

Early Norse carpenters had few tools and no building materials other than wood, stone, and straw. Consequently, they were

forced to build houses as simply as possible. There were no iron hinges; doors usually hung on leather thongs.

Since doors had to be closed in cold weather, some form of ventilation had to be provided. This was usually done by leaving a hole, or "eye," in the roof. Through it, smoke and foul air could escape. Because the wind frequently whistled through it, the air hole was called *vindr auga* (wind eye).

English builders borrowed the Norse term, modified it to *window*, and developed new techniques by which the eye that once admitted the wind now holds it out.

Furniture

War and conquest dominated the thought of the Middle Ages. Artisans and smiths gave a great deal of attention to development of both offensive weapons and defensive armor. Though styles slowly changed, the life of the soldier was likely to depend upon his supply of up-to-date equipment. The early French called a man's warlike equipment his *fourniture,* from their term for "to furnish." Normans took the word to England, where its spelling was slightly altered, but the old meaning was retained. As late as 1603 it was not unusual usage when a traveler described Turkish soldiers as differing from European "in language, countenance, and furniture."

Adoption of modern weapons reduced the amount of hardware carried by soldiers, so the military term was applied to any type of portable equipment. Of these, the articles used to furnish a house were of paramount importance, so *furniture* came to designate portable equipment for any type of building.

Bureau

Curious persons may be inclined to wonder how the word *bureau* came to be applied to such totally unrelated things as a chest of drawers for the bedroom and a department or office of government.

Of French origin, the term at first stood only for a particular kind of coarse red woolen cloth. Bureau was widely used as a cover for both bedroom chests and long tables about which officials sat to conduct business. In time the word came to stand for the furniture covered by the fabric rather than the cloth itself.

From big tables, or bureaus, used by dignitaries assembled in conference session, the name transferred to the group of officials themselves. Since government bureaus are thus literally only red cloth, it is not strange that they have always abounded in red tape.

XVII

HORSE AND RIDER

At the End of One's Rope □ **To Pester** □
Cinch □ **To Ride Roughshod** □ **Posthaste** □ **To
Be Balled Up** □ **To Balk** □ **Spur** □

At the End of One's Rope

Domesticated thousands of years before the beginning of recorded history, horses remained scarce and costly even in classical times. The Greeks valued horses more for their beauty than for their work capacity. Homer and other ancient writers portrayed the horse as a partner of the great hero, so that they had their own equivalent of "a knight in shining armor riding on a white stallion."

Greeks devised the first horse races—riding in chariots rather than saddles. It remained for relatively primitive people, however, to see in the sturdy animal an important military asset. Largely because they had an abundant supply of sturdy short-legged horses, the Huns were better travelers and fighters than most of their competitors. Even the Romans neglected cavalry, and seldom had more than one mounted man to every score of foot soldiers. For this reason some historians insist that the horse was the most important factor in bringing about the decline and final collapse of the Western Roman Empire.

Cavalrymen became the lords of Europe and retained their mastery for more than a thousand years. For merchants and travelers as well as fighting men, a horse might mean the difference between life and death. As a result of its importance, the animal was usually well tended. Many ingenious methods were devised by which riders could give their mounts freedom to graze without being able to escape. But even the most elaborate kinds of hobbles and tethers seldom proved more effective than a length of rope. With one end tied to his bridle and the other to a tree or stump, a horse at the end of his rope could fill his stomach while his master rested. Naturally, many an animal moved as far as he could and then strained his neck to eat grass barely within reach. From this literal usage it became customary to compare a harassed human, one who had exhausted his resources, with a tethered horse.

To Pester

As very often horses strained to graze beyond the reach of a tether, other methods were needed to keep them in place.

Roman farmers discovered that tying a drag behind the horse's hoof and fetlock (above and behind the hoof) worked very well. This was called a pastern hobble (from *pastorium,* meaning "to tether"), and was soon adopted in many regions. From its name Old French used *empester* to express the idea of hobbling while eating. The ancient horse term was abbreviated when it crossed the English Channel and entered modern speech as the verb meaning to bother someone to the point of not letting go.

Cinch

City-bred adventurers who flocked to the gold fields in 1849 encountered many odd customs. Not the least of these was the use of a novel saddle girth. Instead of using English-style bellybands with straps and buckles, Indians and Mexicans of the Southwest employed twisted horsehair ropes running between two rings.

Such a piece of gear, which the Spanish called *cincha,* was far more adjustable than any similar equipment in the East. A rider who knew how to fasten a cinch could lace a saddle on so that it would stay in position all day. Clumsy buckles, on the other hand, had to be adjusted at frequent intervals. Such was the holding power of the *cinch* that its name entered common speech to stand for any sure or easy thing.

To Ride Roughshod

Smiths of the Middle Ages who made and installed horseshoes anticipated the work of modern automobile-tire manufacturers in one respect: They devised a variety of different designs for use under varied conditions.

Almost simultaneously, men working independently in a number of nations had an inspiration. They tried to turn horses into killers by deliberately equipping mounts of cavalrymen with metal shoes that had projecting points or cutting edges.

This idea never worked very well, for a "rough-shod" horse often hit about as many of his rider's comrades as his foes. Nevertheless, to an injured man on the battlefield there wasn't a more fearful sight than that of a big stallion shod for war and about to step on him.

Even though the idea of turning horseshoes into weapons had little effect upon the course of history, *to ride roughshod* remains as a sort of fossil preserved in speech, used to name any violent and brutal conduct toward an opponent already down.

Posthaste

Rapid transmission of important messages has been a matter of concern since early times. Royal couriers were carefully organized in such diverse lands as China, Mexico, and ancient Persia. Before the beginning of the present era, Greeks and Romans had elaborate systems to handle imperial letters.

Ordinary folk could not avail themselves of such facilities, though. Under leadership of the University of Paris, the world's first public mail service was launched in the thirteenth century. Men and horses were kept at special places; from the Latin word for "station," such a point was called a post. The English borrowed the post system and used it first for transmission of the king's packet. By 1635 it was so widely used on the island that regular rates for public correspondence were established.

Persons seldom wrote letters unless they considered them important, and they were always eager to speed them on their journey. So it became a common practice to write across the face of a letter, "Haste, post, haste!" Riders of the post actually did cut quite dashing figures as they sped along on their fine horses. From the actual speed of the post, plus hopes of letter writers, *posthaste* came to mean "in a hurry"—whether connected with letters or not.

To Be Balled Up

Until the present century, a snowbound householder who wished to go for supplies or fetch a doctor was dependent upon the horse for transportation. Even sturdy animals frequently had difficulty, especially when snow was sticky enough to pack. When it became "balled up" under a horse's hooves, he made slow progress. Sometimes he floundered about, hardly able to walk

Spreading from frontier talk into general use, the expression *to be balled up* came to stand for any baffled or helpless condition.

To Balk

Throughout much of northern Europe, early farmers used un-plowed strips of land as dividers between fields. Ridges of this sort served to separate the rows of one man from those of his neighbors. From a word linked with the idea of missing or avoiding, the ribbon of earth avoided by the plow was called a balk.

Naturally, the act of leaving a balk was important. It even had a loose legal significance. So the name became associated with other kinds of avoidance and refusals, such as the jerk made by a horse in turning away from an outstretched bridle. By the time Pizarro began plundering the riches of South America in the sixteenth century, any animal or person who avoided a duty was said *to balk*.

Spur

Until long after the collapse of the Roman Empire, western Europe had comparatively few domestic animals. Meat was greatly in demand for food, but much of it had to be secured by hunting. Hence, most hunters developed a skill in following the spoor of wild animals. Their term for a talon or claw making marks on the ground was the great-grandfather of the modern *spur*.

As early as the eighth century, horsemen developed a metal claw to which they gave the spur's name. Development of the term was slow for the next seven hundred years. Then the tremendous popularity of fighting cocks armed with steel gaffs, or spurs, brought new vitality to the word.

Early railroaders had no standard term for short lengths of track leading off a main line. Then someone compared such a section with the spur of a game rooster, and the name stuck. By 1878 a newspaper reporter did not have to explain his meaning when he referred to "a spur leading to the Great Northern." Spreading from the lingo of English railroaders, the term became standard throughout the Western world.

XVIII

SCIENCE AND INVENTION

To Have a Screw Loose □ Camera □ Watch □ Patent □ Iodine □ Satellite □ Siren □ Pliers □ Countdown □

To Have a Screw Loose

Cotton has been an item of world trade for centuries. But it did not gain its commanding position until the invention of machinery with which to process it. Several of the most important devices were perfected in quick succession late in the eighteenth century.

Richard Arkwright patented his roller spinning frame in 1769, and the following year James Hargreaves devised the spinning jenny. Using it as a model, Samuel Crompton (1753–1827) invented the greatly improved industrial mule, or muslin wheel. All these machines were soon operated by power from Watt's steam engine, and by 1785 the power loom was in use.

Use of cotton increased at a fantastic rate—7,500 percent in seventy years. Mills multiplied, and owners hired the cheapest possible labor. Machines were frequently tended by young children, and the few mechanics were usually inexperienced. This combination resulted in frequent breakdowns. Even when all the looms were running, it seemed that one or more was always producing defective cloth.

Such behavior was usually blamed on a loose screw somewhere in the machine. So by the early 1800s, a person who wished to indicate that something was wrong with the behavior of a mechanism or a person would remark that there was a screw loose somewhere.

Camera

Workmen of ancient Rome built many an arched vault, which they called a *camera,* from a Greek term for ''curved.'' Popular usage eventually made the term stand for any type of chamber.

With that meaning in mind, English scientists of the sixteenth century borrowed the old Latin word. They had discovered that a convex lens fixed in one end of a darkened room could be made to throw the image of an external object on the opposite wall. They knew of no practical use for such a dark chamber, but gave it a sonorous Latin name—*camera obscura*.

Eventually a miniature *camera obscura* was devised. Small enough to be carried from place to place, it was a sealed box with a lens in one end and a view hole in the top. Artists used it in sketching, but no one had any idea that the little dark chamber would ever have commercial importance.

In 1802, Thomas Wedgwood, the son of Josiah Wedgwood, a famous potter, had an inspiration. It was known that light rays affect silver compounds. Inventors had made many attempts to devise a method of bringing an image to focus upon a layer of metal in such a fashion that a picture would be burned into it. Wedgwood decided to place a light-sensitive plate into a *camera obscura*. He produced silhouette pictures, but they faded quickly unless they were kept in the dark. Thomas Wedgwood's experiments with the little dark chamber proved that photography was more than an idle dream, and the *camera* entered a new phase of its long history.

Watch

Among major inventions of the early Middle Ages was a workable type of spring drive for small mechanisms that was gradually adapted to a widening circle of devices. Finally someone thought of using it for timepieces, and clumsy iron-cased pocket clocks began to be seen.

These portable clocks proved especially valuable for use by civic patrols. Carrying one of them, the watchman—or watch—could make his rounds on a definite schedule. This device was so widely adopted by guardians of the peace that it took the name of the officer who carried it and entered modern speech as the *watch*.

Patent

European rulers of the late Middle Ages had dictatorial power over practically every area of life. If a sovereign wished, he could grant one of his favorites a vast tract of land, a title, or even the right to a monopoly in some type of trade. Such privileges were commonly listed in an official document which the owner could exhibit in order to prove his claims. To distinguish papers of this sort from such secret transactions as treaties, they were called *lettres patents* (open letters).

Abbreviated to *patent,* the royal grant was later attached to products of inventive genius. The first patent issued by the United States government was to Samuel Hopkins of Vermont on July 31, 1790, for a process by which he made potash and pearl ashes. Only three patents were issued that year. Among the first of modern patents was a secret formula for making leather waterproof by means of a shiny black varnish. Varieties of this "patent-treated leather" were in use as early as 1800. It proved so popular that the name was clipped to *patent* and applied not only to varnished leather but also to manufactured fabrics of similar appearance.

Iodine

Joseph Louis Gay-Lussac (1778–1850), the most noted French chemist of his generation, was the natural person to consult about any odd substance. One of his fellow scientists experimenting with ashes from burned seaweed had isolated a strange grayish-black solid. He had no idea what it might be or whether it would prove of any use, so he sent a specimen to the Sorbonne.

There, Gay-Lussac studied the queer stuff and concluded it to be a new element. At ordinary temperatures he found it to behave in staid fashion, but when he heated a quantity to 185 degrees, it changed to a strange blue-violet vapor. There was a striking resemblance between the color of the odd gas and that of the chemist's favorite flower, the violet.

It was customary to base scientific names upon Greek words. So the Frenchman took *iode*, the classical name for the common violet, and bestowed it upon his discovery. Sir Humphrey Davy, experimenting with *iode*, found it to have many valuable properties. Its flower-based name modified to *iodine*, the new chemical became a standard weapon in the war against bacteria.

Satellite

No other city, ancient or modern, can be compared with Rome in terms of world domination. For a period of more than a thousand years the metropolis was the hub of Western civilization. Eventually, however, the very life of the Empire was threatened by economic unrest and a series of rapid changes in government.

Matters reached such a state that no person of importance dared walk the streets of the capital without an escort. Many notables were literally surrounded by armed bodyguards; members of such a guard were known as satellites, from an old name for an "attendant."

Despite their satellites, one aristocrat after another was murdered. External difficulties multiplied, the Empire crashed, and classical Latin ceased to be the language of commerce and science. But learned men revived the ancient tongue ten centuries later and used it for most formal speech. Among the resurrected terms was *satellite*, which medieval rulers applied to their personal guards.

Johannes Kepler (1571–1630) thought of the king's satellites when he heard about the strange bodies revolving about Jupiter. Discovered by Galileo, the secondary planets hovered about the planet like guards and courtiers encircling a prince. So in 1611 Kepler named them *satellites;* soon the term was applied to all heavenly bodies that revolve about primary masses.

Siren

Baron Cagnard de la Tour, an obsure French scientist, was fascinated by problems connected with sound. In 1819 he succeeded in making a revolving plate with which he could measure vibrations of musical notes. At certain speeds the strange device produced sounds similar to the human voice, and a particularly sweet tone resulted when it was partly immersed in water.

Casting about for a suitable name for his invention, the baron turned to classical mythology. Greek tales included many references to the siren—a sweet-singing half-woman, half-fish whose voice frequently lured seamen to destruction. Since his invention also sang in the water, de la Tour called it the siren. His principle was soon utilized to produce large-scale devices for giving fog warnings to steamships. Eventually *siren* became the standard name for any noisemaker that serves to give warning—thereby reversing ancient usage, according to which songs of the siren attracted all who heard them.

Pliers

Manufacture of metal tools proceeded slowly throughout the Middle Ages. Though individual craftsmen developed great skill in shaping soft metals, especially gold, metallurgy had not yet reached a point where steel devices could be produced in quantity. Not until about the time of Columbus's first voyage to the New World did smiths devise a small steel tool for handling and shaping. Modeled after the tongs of the blacksmith, it was used for bending and holding. So it was called pliers, from the French word *plieur* (folder).

Spelling remained haphazard for generations; a record book dated 1569 records the purchase of "a pair of plyars" at sixpence. By the late seventeenth century, both flat and round-nosed types were in common use, but it remained for modern manufacturing methods to multiply both supply and demand for numerous special types of *pliers.*

Countdown

As strange as it may seem, the creator of the countdown technique used during launchings was a motion-picture director named Fritz Lang. Lang directed one of the very earliest science-fiction films in the late 1920s, titled *The Girl in the Moon.* One of the major scenes in the movie was the launching of a huge rocket. It occurred to Lang that greater suspense could be built by switching from the normal "one, two, three . . . " to exactly the reverse. Later science decided to imitate the director's *countdown* idea.

XIX

TRAVEL AND TRANSPORTATION

To Railroad □ Highway □ To String Along □ To Go Through Customs □ To Make the Grade □ To Break the Ice □ Jaywalker □ Middle-of-the-Road □ Cabby □ To Sidetrack □ To Give the Gun □

To Railroad

Until the advent of the automobile, horse-drawn carriages had no challengers except the railroads. Trains hauled hundreds of tons of cargo with ease. As early as 1837, the *North Star* locomotive broke all records by plunging down the rails at sixty miles per hour. So it was proverbial that anything connected with the railroad was likely to be big and fast.

That tradition was upheld by one of America's most colorful construction jobs. In 1864, major interests pressed for action on the daring project of laying ribbons of steel from the Atlantic to the Pacific. Five frantic years followed. Working from both ends, the Union Pacific and the Central Pacific extended tracks toward each other. They eventually met at Promontory, Utah. But in order to do so, workmen had had to push across rivers, through forests, and over mountains. No matter what the obstacles, the railroad had to be built—in a hurry.

Pell-mell overriding of difficulties became so linked with construction of railroads that a new phrase was born. Any person or group pushing a program or idea without regard for opposition is said *to railroad* it through.

Highway

Old English, a guttural language, was quite unlike modern speech. Among its common words was *heah*—used to mean both "tall" and "chief." Thus a stag was called heah deor (high deer) and an important town official was called a heah burh (chief burough).

Roads of the era fell into two major classes. There were many narrow trails that wound across private estates of noblemen and were not open to general travel. Towns were usually connected by public roads maintained by officers of the king. Such a road was called a heah-way, because it was a chief road by comparison with the private trail, or by-way.

Emerging into modern speech as *highway,* the term was long used to stand for any major route by either water or land. Only within the last century, under the impact of the automobile, has the name come to be reserved for a land route suitable for high-speed travel.

To String Along

Almost from the time men first employed halters and bridles with their beasts of burden, strings of them were formed for some operations. Caravan drivers tied as many as fifty camels together in single file, then handled them with only two or three men. Long strings of mules were linked in pack trains, and smaller groups of horses were often driven in the same fashion.

It was difficult and sometimes impossible to handle a fine saddle horse in this way, however. Snorting and bucking, he would refuse to follow in the docile fashion of a pack animal. Any person who agrees *to string along* with the crowd instead of going his own way is actually comparing himself with a meek beast of burden!

To Go Through Customs

The modern customs station derives its name from an Old French term *custume*—equivalent to costume, or habitual mode of dress. This label was used so frequently that it attached to any common practice or usage, whether involving clothing or not.

One such common practice was that of collecting rents, dues, and taxes. Lords and rulers were careful to see that no one failed

to pay customary charges, hence any levy exacted as a matter of course came to be known as a custom.

Several centuries ago, European kings adopted the ancient practice of exacting a charge as a condition for permitting merchants to pass through certain cities on trade routes. In order to collect customary passage fees officers had to be employed. In order to function they had to have regular stations. So by the time Columbus discovered America, the customhouse was a familiar European institution.

As the base of international travel broadened, it was natural to have officers check the luggage of tourists as well as assess taxes upon merchants' goods. In popular speech the old word for a habitual tax was slurred into plural form, with the result that it is now customary for persons who cross national boundaries *to go through customs.*

To Make the Grade

Total railroad trackage in the United States in 1830 was less than forty miles. Once the iron horse proved his might, however, investors began a frantic period of expansion. More than 150,000 miles of lines were completed in half a century.

It was already well known that the pulling power of a locomotive is greatly affected by the slope, or grade, of a piece of track. Nearly five times as much steam is required when a train moves from straight, level sections to a grade that slopes as little as 1 percent.

Hasty and sometimes careless engineering led builders to include some grades so steep that they challenged the power of engines. Trainmen were always elated when they succeeded in reaching the top of a difficult pull. Consequently, any person who wins against heavy obstacles is compared with a puffing engine and said *to make the grade.*

To Break the Ice

London owes much of her place in history to the river that flows through the city. The Thames, big enough for major shipping but tame by comparison with those of swift current, became a major artery of commerce many centuries ago.

The docks of London are some forty miles from the river's mouth at Southend. Tides affect the water level but push little brine into the river. Therefore, in severe winter weather, ice is a major nuisance to operators of small boats. Until the development of power equipment, it was frequently necessary to chop with hand tools in order to make channels for plying about the river's edge.

This operation was by no means confined to London and environs. It constituted the boatman's preliminary work. He had *to break the ice* before he could actually get down to business. Drifting from docks and wharves, the river-born expression came to indicate any method of making a start.

Jaywalker

The blue jay, seldom seen in the Old World, attracted many comments from early settlers in America. Noisy and boisterous, the bird abounded along the eastern seaboard.

As villages grew into cities, the jays retreated farther into the country. Consequently, the colorful birds came to be associated with life in sparsely settled areas. They were so characteristic of the country that it was natural to link them with persons who lived there. By the middle of the nineteenth century, *jay* was in wide use as a colloquial synonym for "hick." College upperclassmen used it to refer to freshmen, and city slickers applied it to country cousins.

Jays were a source of considerable amusement when they

ventured into the larger cities. Ignorant of traffic laws, they blithely crossed against signals; frequently they ignored corners and cut across diagonally. Such careless walking was so strongly associated with countryfolk that any pedestrian who violated traffic regulations came to be called a *jaywalker*.

Middle-of-the-Road

Few great roads were built in America until a generation after the Civil War. Even a road between major cities was likely to be narrow and poorly tended. Constant pressure from wagon and carriage wheels kept the edges of one-way roads cut well below the level of the middle. This meant that in wet weather, a man who didn't want to get his feet muddy had to walk in the middle of the road.

Late in the century, many cautious members of the Popularist party opposed union with the Democrats. They wished to take a safe middle ground between the two extremes then supported by political opponents. Someone mockingly referred to the cautious ones as members of the Middle-of-the-Road party. This label stuck, and *middle-of-the-road* has remained in common use long after the cautious Popularists were forgotten.

Cabby

About two hundred years ago an unknown Italian craftsman perfected an odd new vehicle. The light two-wheeled chaise drawn by one horse bounded over obstacles almost like a goat leaping among rocks. So *capra*, the name of the he-goat, attached to the sprightly device. It was later adopted by the French and the title was modified to *cabriolet*.

It soon became immensely popular. An English traveler writing from Paris in 1789 complained vigorously. These infernal one-passenger vehicles, said he, made it dangerous to venture on foot at any hour. Nevertheless, they soon crossed the Channel. In England the name of the dashing vehicles was abbreviated to *cab*. It made such a success that the label was attached to many types of horsedrawn conveyances; it then passed on to mean only autos for hire.

Development of the complex stream of speech halted for a time. Then jocular American patrons linked *cab* and *driver* and gave the vehicle's name to him. *Cabby* closely resembles *capra*, Italian for the he-goat whose antics named ancestors of the cab. So the label entitles your favorite cabby to keep on cavorting through traffic like a frisky goat.

To Sidetrack

When we say we have been *sidetracked*, or *gotten off the track*, we are, in fact, tracing American vocabulary to terminology we have inherited from our transportation system. Big in growth, with land to conquer and coasts to link, America depended on the railroad. And because so many Americans found their livelihoods through the iron horse, it is not surprising that we should see remnants of this cultural upheaval in our language today.

To sidetrack, for example, was a way to allow one train to move on while another waited for repairs, or in abeyance. Colloquially, it has come down to us as a way of saying that we have been interrupted from concentrating on our major concerns.

To Give the Gun

Students of word ways have found it difficult to account for the use of *to give the gun* as a way of saying "to accelerate." Early quotations are lacking, and the only reasonable explanation connects the expression with World War I.

Combat planes of the period were slow and clumsy. In attacking an enemy it was standard practice to climb above him and dive to gain speed. Giving his engine all the gas it would take, the pilot would open up with his machine gun. This led to the association of rapid acceleration with gunning. After becoming fixed in the speech of airmen, the expression was soon applied to automobiles and speedboats as well.

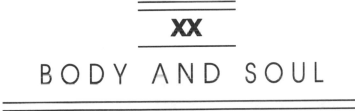

XX

BODY AND SOUL

To Throw into Stitches □ **Brainstorm** □ **Apple of the Eye** □ **Charley Horse** □ **To Have One's Heart in the Right Place** □ **A Nose for Trouble** □ **Goose Pimples** □ **Cold-Blooded** □ **A Skeleton in the Closet** □ **Hand to Mouth** □

To Throw into Stitches

The speech of several early Teutonic peoples included forms of a word meaning "to stick," as with the point of a knife. Passing through Old English as *stice,* it was later modified to *stitch.*

One characteristic stablike pain, caused by acute spasms of rib muscles, is especially prominent after strenuous exercise. Though no wound is involved, one may hurt almost as though actually stabbed. Athletes—especially runners—are still prone to pains from such a "stitch" in the side.

Long ago it was noticed that strong and prolonged laughter may lead to a stabbing muscular cramp. So the designation for a minor knife wound came to be used for pains caused by excessive hilarity. It clings in speech with such persistence that any unusually funny story is still said *to throw* readers or listeners *into stitches.*

Brainstorm

Mankind has always been fascinated by the strange and occult. Folktales and scholarly inquiries alike have come to focus upon such matters as hypnosis, divination, dowsing, clairvoyance, and communication by strange mental processes.

F.W.H. Myers, a distinguished English leader of investigators in such fields, became greatly interested in what he called telepathy. In 1882, he founded the now-famous Society for Psychical Research, which made a determined effort to conduct investigations in a scientific fashion. Though it provoked both criticism and ridicule, the movement became the talk of Europe and America. Many enthusiasts compared telepathy with radio and suggested that it rests upon the action of brainwaves.

Engineers already knew that electrical storms affect many types of communication; it was an easy step to compare a disturbed radio with a chaotic mind. On the basis of that metaphor, a person suffering temporary mental derangement was said to be in a brainstorm. Not all brainstorms are pathological, however. Many inventions, literary masterpieces, and other works have come from persons excited to the point of seeming slightly unbalanced. So the expression was attached to the turbulent process of getting a new idea, and the man or woman who produces one is likely to credit it to a still-mysterious *brainstorm.*

Apple of the Eye

There is a great deal of evidence to indicate that apples were eaten many thousands of years ago. If not the very first, this fruit was among the earliest of those which became a favorite with humans. Charred remains of apples have been found in prehistoric sites such as Swiss lake dwellings.

People of early Israel were well acquainted with the apple. It was so familiar that they applied its name to the human eye—which is shaped quite like a round pippin. So they often spoke of ''the apple of the eye.''

Scrupture frequently stresses the supreme value of the eyes in passages like Deuteronomy 32:10, Psalms 17:8, and Proverbs 7:2. With fine shades of meaning lost in translation, English Bibles include a number of references to the fruitlike organ—which resulted in anything extremely precious, no matter what its shape, being termed *the apple of the eye.*

Charley Horse

Long after it had become a great city, London was a haven for thugs and criminals. Charles I became alarmed over the situation, and in 1640 ordered a sweeping extension of police powers. His new watchmen were the butt of many an underworld joke. From the king's name rogues called an officer Charley's man, or simply Charley.

Once established in slang, the title proved to have surprising vitality. It attached to all constables and local police and was in wide use among American lawbreakers of the nineteenth century. Since it was customary for the Charley to make his beat on foot, flat feet and aching legs were common occupational maladies of peace officers.

Rise of big-time baseball produced a crop of athletes who suffered from similar ailments. Any player who developed a muscular cramp, which was especially likely to strike the legs, was compared with a watchman and said to be weary from riding "Charley's horse." From that usage it was a short step to call the stiff muscle itself a *Charley horse*. The *Cincinnati Commercial Gazette* commented in 1889 that a certain "Mac" had developed a Charley horse which ended his ballplaying the previous season.

To Have One's Heart in the Right Place

Egyptian priests who worked as embalmers were probably the first group of persons to have an accurate knowledge of the heart's size and location. Long before the beginning of the Christian era, these specialists knew that the heart is a cone-shaped organ about the size of one's fist. They also knew that it always lies in the thoracic cavity between the lungs and just behind the breastbone.

Much knowledge was lost with the decay of ancient civilizations, yet since the thirteenth century, when scientific anatomy became an official science, educated men have had a fairly accurate understanding of the body's pumping organ.

Neither ancient lore nor more recent discoveries have had the slightest effect upon speech customs, which have regarded the heart as a wandering rather than a fixed organ. A fearful person was long described as having his heart in his mouth. An easily offended person is still said to wear his heart on his sleeve.

Late in the seventeenth century, another descriptive phrase surged into wide use, and in the space age it shows no indication of dropping out of our speech. For in spite of the findings of anatomists, it seems reasonable to say that anyone with good intentions is properly made and therefore *has his heart in the right place*.

A Nose for Trouble

Much evidence suggests that the sense of smell once dominated the brains of most higher animals. When the animal kingdom as a whole is considered, it is still probably the most effective means of gaining information about the outside world.

A dog's olfactory apparatus dominates much of his brain, and many of his instincts and reflexes relate to his sense of smell. Even fish literally follow their noses. Salmon headed upstream will turn back from water saturated with odors produced by men or bears.

The nose of man is primarily an air vent. His external organs of smell, about the size of a fingernail, are far inside the nose. Hence, ordinary air currents do not flow directly over them in breathing, and it is necessary for us to make a deliberate effort to sniff when we wish to analyze an odor.

Range of sensitivity to odors is very wide, however, and some people respond readily to scents that others cannot detect by deliberate effort.

Capacity to anticipate the course of events is also a major variable. Some people show little or no sensitivity to impending difficulties while others have uncanny skill in recognizing that trouble is coming. Common folk, baffled by this important and highly complex variable, have often taken the easy way out and explained it as due to differences in keenness of smell. In almost every area of human endeavor, a person with an unusual capacity for detecting impending difficulties is said by his admiring associates to have *a nose for trouble*.

Goose Pimples

Geese played an important part in the life of medieval Britain as well as other European countries. A prosperous farmer in some English counties—notably Norfolk and Lincoln—was likely to keep a thousand adult birds. Each produced on the average about seven goslings a year.

Flocks were regularly taken to pasture and water, much in the fashion of sheep. It was therefore logical that the man who tended them should be known as a gooseherd. In autumn, birds were driven to market in London, waddling along at about one mile an hour.

Good strains of geese produced so many feathers that they were usually plucked five times a year. With its soft, downy covering removed, a near-naked goose reacted quickly to any drop in temperature.

Like many other birds, the goose is equipped with an elaborate network of muscles whose purpose is to pull feathers erect and form a "dead air" blanket. This natural insulation system is activated by thousands of tiny muscles in the skin that contract at the first breath of cold air.

Plucked geese react just like fully feathered ones—with the important difference that the skin reactions of bare fowls are clearly visible. From gooseherd to housewife and from broker to farm boy, everyone was familiar with the queer, pimpled skin of a plucked goose exposed to the cold. The bodily reactions of humans in response to a draft, with the same involuntary contractions of tiny muscles, despite the scanty hair on the body, were long ago seen to be much like those of geese. That being the case, it was natural that the minute bumps raised on human skin should be called *goose pimples*.

Cold-blooded

Blood has been a source of fascination and mystery for untold centuries. Many ancient and primitive religions included rites in which blood was central. Galen, a noted Greek doctor of the second century, considered it to be a "living" fluid, the very seat of life.

Everyday experience suggests that there are strong links between the state of one's blood and his emotions. During anger or after activity, sensations in the face and neck hint that the vital fluid has become warmer. And the feelings that accompany acute fear can be interpreted to mean that the temperature of the blood has suddenly dropped.

Medieval scholars noticed that temperaments differ. Some persons are easily goaded into a rage—becoming so furious that their blood seems to reach the boiling point. Others seldom lose their tranquillity. A person of the latter type was considered to be without passion, or cold-blooded. Precisely the same notion is preserved in the French word *sangfroid*.

Modern physiology has exploded the myth of wide variations in blood temperature, but the influence of the past is too strong for reforms in speech. Though we know a thermometer would show the fluid in his veins to be 98.6 degrees or thereabouts—quite warm—we still classify a cruel or vindictive person as cold-blooded.

A Skeleton in the Closet

Scientific study of human anatomy is a very recent development. Ancient doctors refused to cut into a corpse for fear of the ghost of the deceased. This fear gradually mellowed into a kind of "respect for the dead," so firmly fixed that English law prohibited surgeons from practicing dissection. There was only one loophole

in the law: A doctor might cut up the body of an executed criminal. This condition prevailed until passage of the Anatomy Act of 1832, which was a statute authorizing and regulating the study of anatomy and the disposition of dead bodies.

But the rise of modern medicine created a great demand for anatomical subjects. Professional grave robbers, or "resurrection men," dug up bodies and sold them to physicians at high prices. Many an early doctor dissected only one body in his life. Naturally he would prize the skeleton highly and be reluctant to dispose of it. But public opinion made it dangerous for him to keep it where it might be found. So the prudent anatomist usually hung his prize in some dark corner where visitors were not likely to see it.

This practice was so common that people began to take it for granted that a doctor had *a skeleton in his closet*. From this literal sense the phrase eventually came to indicate any hidden evidence.

Hand to Mouth

Modern agriculture has not entirely conquered hunger, but except for the Irish potato famine of 1846, the Western world has known few real famines since the sixteenth century. In that era one disaster followed another. It seemed that things could not possibly get worse; then in 1586 grain crops failed throughout Great Britain.

Thousands of people actually starved to death. Multitudes became thin from hunger. Food was so scarce that when a person managed to get a bit, he was likely to eat it on the spot. As soon as he had a piece of bread in his hand, he would thrust into his mouth. Such *hand-to-mouth* existence was so common that the phrase came to be used of any substandard living condition.

XXI

POLITICS AND GOVERNMENT

Heckle □ Slate □ Filibuster □ To Lean over Backward □ Spellbinder □ Dark Horse □ Also-ran □ Idiot □ All Over but the Shouting □ To Spill the Beans □ Lobby □ Haul over the Coals □ Great Scott □ Uncle Sam □

Heckle

Flax was the chief vegetable fiber used in medieval cloth making. Though the fibers are long and strong, their preparation presented many problems to the prescientific age. Stalks were first permitted to putrefy; then they were split and combed by hand.

A brush with iron teeth was used for the latter operation. The instrument was known as a heckle, from the Anglo-Saxon term *hecel* (to split). By the fifteenth century the word had come to be used as a verb meaning "to scratch with a steel brush," or "to look for weak points."

Scottish candidates for public office were customarily subjected to public questioning. Voters were merciless in looking for weak points in those whom they opposed. So *heckle* was borrowed from the flax floor and applied to any disturbance intended to distract a public speaker.

Slate

Slate was in wide use as a writing material as early as the fourteenth century. It became standard equipment for all occasions on which temporary notices were displayed.

Among others, political leaders found it very useful. Groups of party officials conferring about their list of nominees would place a large slate before the house. Names were listed, erased, and substituted until general agreement was reached. Current in the Untied States as late as 1800, this use of the black writing surface caused any list of candidates to be called a *slate*.

Filibuster

Many United States citizens believe it is beneath the dignity of Congress to permit a minority group to delay action by means of a filibuster. On etymological grounds they are probably right—for the word is a survival of the lawless days of the Spanish Main.

Bearded cutthroats who preyed on shipping of all nations were known to the British as freebooters, buccaneers, or pirates. But for such ruffians the French had only the term *flibustier,* meaning "free booty." Adopted into English with slight modifications in spelling, the pirate word became *filibuster.*

To Lean over Backward

As late as the eighteenth century, legal scales were weighted against accused persons. English judges of the period gained a reputation for especially high-handed administration of justice. Many of these officials gained their appointments through political influence and were notorious for "leaning"—showing open prejudice in favor of the prosecution. This was especially marked in cases of treason, for condemned traitors forfeited all their property to the crown.

Vigorous clean-up campaigns led to a period of careful appointments. Many new justices were alert to the civil rights of accused persons. To avoid any suggestion of leaning toward the crown, some of them went to opposite extremes. Such an overly conscientious judge was said *to lean over backward,* and the phrase came to stand for any stickler who went beyond the letter of the law.

Spellbinder

Few United States political campaigns have been so hectic as that of 1888. It is best known as the race in which Grover Cleveland

won a popular majority of 100,000 votes—only to lose the office to Benjamin Harrison by the action of the electoral college.

As early as July of that year, it was apparent that the major parties were closely balanced. Since the Democratic incumbent was running for reelection, he had a slight edge. But small parties such as Union Labor, Prohibition, and American counted enough members to swing the election. Consequently, leaders of the Republican campaign set out to capture the independent and small-party vote.

Noted men arranged long and intense speaking tours, and oratory was dished out with a lavish hand. Republican editors were uniformly enthusiastic in their reports of rallies and described many a party spokesman as holding the audience as though bound in a spell. This phrase caught the popular fancy, and there was some talk of a permanent "Republican Spellbinders Association." It was generally conceded that platform oratory was the factor that led to Republican gains, so *spellbinder* entered common speech as a title for any overpersuasive speaker.

Dark Horse

From the beginning of the democratic experiment, the election of public officials has been recognized to have quite a lot in common with a horse race. Nobody knows just who is going to win before the votes are counted, but everybody has a favorite for whom he's pulling. So no disparagement is intended when a public figure compares a candidate with a spirited nag.

No less a person than James Buchanan predicted two years before General Zachary Taylor's election to the presidency that "if the war were over and Taylor nominated by the Whigs, he would be a hard horse to beat."

There's a possibility that the comparison between competitors on the track and at the polls was influenced by a Tennessee horse trader. Legend has it that Sam Flynn picked up an easy living by racing a coal-black stallion named Dusky Pete. According to this account, Flynn usually rode Dusky Pete into a strange town as though he were an ordinary saddle horse. Not knowing they faced a veteran runner, local men cheerfully set up races—and lost. As a result, Flynn's dark horse became more than locally noted.

No doubt the formation of the new political term was helped by the fact that anything dark is foreboding and unlikely. At any rate, lingo of the track entered smoke-filled convention halls with the result that any political unknown who shows a chance of being elected is termed a *dark horse*.

Also-ran

In most horse races, judges do not determine the order in which all the animals finish. They simply clock the first three across the line.

Newspapers of the last century naturally gave prominence to horses that placed in important races. They frequently described all three animals, gave their time, and listed their owners and winnings. Toward the end of such a story it was customary to mention horses that also ran.

During the third quarter of the century, United States presidential elections came to resemble horse races. Many new parties were organized: Greenback, Anti-Monopoly, United Labor, National Silver, Prohibition, American, and others. Their candidates seldom gave any serious competition to men selected by old-line parties. So after elections, newspapers dismissed many an obscure aspirant for the presidency as an *also-ran*—one who didn't come close enough to winning to have his order determined. By the turn of the century the expression had come to be applied to any person badly beaten in competition of any sort.

Idiot

No civilization, ancient or modern, has had a more exalted idea of civic responsibility than did early Greece. There, the highest honor that could come to a citizen was a place of public trust—even though no pay might be involved.

A man who held no office was called *idios* (private). Eventually the word came to be applied to persons mentally incapable of taking part in community affairs. Then, slightly modified in spelling, its meaning was again broadened—to stand for any individual with less than normal intelligence.

Which serves as a vivid reminder that, even now, only an *idiot* will ignore the opportunities and responsibilities of citizenship.

All Over but the Shouting

General use of printed tickets or ballots has become standard election practice only in recent centuries. Under English common law it was long customary to submit many local issues to voice vote. Citizens assembled on a specified day, then expressed their will by shouting for the proposal or candidate they favored.

Noise was so intimately associated with these occasions that the election itself came to be known as a shouting. It was not unusual for a campaign to be conducted with such fervor that the outcome became clear before the day of the shouting. In such an instance it was literally *all over but the shouting*. Applied to contests in general, the political term came to name any situation where victory is clear before a final decision is reached.

To Spill the Beans

Early Greek secret societies had very strict membership requirements. A candidate for admission was voted upon by the members, and only a few adverse ballots were required to disqualify him.

In order to keep the voting secret, white beans were dropped into a jar or helmet by those favoring the candidate, while brown or black beans constituted negative votes. Only officials of the group were supposed to know how many adverse votes were cast, but occasionally a clumsy voter, dropping his bean into the jar, would knock it over and disclose its contents to onlookers.

To spill the beans in the literal fashion was embarrassing, to say the least. Medieval scholars who delved into the cultures of Greece and Rome translated the ancient term for clumsiness into a figurative phrase naming indiscretion in revealing information of any sort.

Lobby

Most major buildings of medieval times were constructed in the interests of the Church. Community life frequently centered about the monastery, where persons went for medicine, legal advice, letter writing, and many other activities, in addition to spiritual guidance. So numerous were visitors that it was often necessary for some of them to wait outside the building in the *lobia,* or vine-covered walk, that led into the monastery. It seems to have taken its name from the old German word *laubo,* which meant "leafy."

As other types of public buildings were developed, architects frequently included a waiting room. Though covered with a roof instead of leaves, it retained the name of the monastery's walkway. Spelling was modified when the word was adopted into English, and it entered modern speech as *lobby.*

United States law forbids persons to go upon the floor of Congress in an attempt to influence lawmakers. Consequently, the lobby soon came to be the place where special interests exerted political pressure. Present-day lobbyists seldom actually work in the lobby; they seek to win votes and influence congressmen in hotels, restaurants, and anywhere else they can find them.

Haul over the Coals

Trial by jury has come into wide use only in modern times. During the Middle Ages it was customary to test an accused person by making him go through some dreadful ordeal. This was done with the idea that God would protect the innocent but permit the guilty to suffer physical harm.

A common form of such trial was the ordeal by fire. Red-hot plowshares were sometimes placed in a row. More often, a bed of coals was prepared. While it still glowed, the accused was forced to walk barefoot across the inferno. If he stumbled and burned to death, he was pronounced guilty. But if he succeeded in crossing the coals, he was acquitted.

It meant extreme danger and fearful pain to be *hauled over the coals*. Even if the man survived, he never forgot his fearful ordeal. Hence, this phrase for a severe testing remains in the language centuries after the barbarous ordeal by fire was abandoned.

Great Scott

Just prior to the Civil War the American political pot was boiling furiously. The Whigs were making a last desperate bid for supremacy and in the election of 1852 were eager to offer a colorful candidate for the presidency.

Winfield Scott seemed to be just the man. He had been made a brigadier general at age twenty-eight. In the thirty years that followed, he had become one of the best-known military leaders in the country. As a commander in the Mexican War, he had captured Vera Cruz and occupied Mexico City. If any Whig could be elected president, it was Winfield Scott.

Offered the nomination, Scott accepted eagerly. He campaigned with a swagger unmatched in American political history. The general was very vain and pompous and his subordinates had long called him "Old Fuss and Feathers"; now his political opponents began to jeer at him as "Great Scott." He was defeated in the election by Franklin Pierce, but the phrase *Great Scott* entered our language as an expression of surprise or disgust.

Uncle Sam

This term came into use during the War of 1812 and was born in Troy, New York. The government inspector there was "Uncle" Sam Wilson, and when the war opened, Elbert Anderson, the contractor in New York, bought a large amount of beef, pork, and pickles for the army. These were inspected by Wilson, and were duly stamped "E.A.—U.S.," meaning "Elbert Anderson, for the United States." The term *U.S.* for the United States was then somewhat new, and the workmen concluded that it referred to Uncle Sam Wilson. After they discovered their mistake, they kept the name up as a joke. These same men soon went to war, where they repeated the joke. It got into print and made the rounds. From that time on, the term *Uncle Sam* was used facetiously for the United States, and it now represents the nation.

XXII

EDUCATION AND SCHOOL

Sheepskin □ **Faculty** □ **Commencement** □
Poser □ **Alphabet** □ **Academy** □ **To Burn the**
Midnight Oil □ **Crisscross** □ **Snob** □

Sheepskin

Long before the beginning of recorded history, men learned to use tanned animal skins for a variety of purposes. Goatskin has usually been less abundant then sheepskin, and is considered inferior for many purposes.

Sheepskin played an important role in the making of clothing as late as the thirteenth century. Much earlier it was used in the form of parchment. Books were bound in it, drumheads were covered by it, and military men even devised sheepskin gear with which to protect fine weapons.

Institutional resistance to change caused colleges and universities to cling to the custom of preparing sheepskin diplomas long after good paper became abundant and cheap. Not only was the actual skin of the animal used; as late as the middle of the nineteenth century, most diplomas were written in Latin.

Whether or not he could read the roll of parchment that certified he had won his degree, a college graduate of the era regarded this very special sheepskin as one of his most important possessions. Born as a slang expression among American students, this vivid name for a diploma has spread around the world and remains very much alive in spite of the fact that most of them are now machine-printed on heavy paper rather than hand-lettered on genuine parchment.

Faculty

From Latin for "power or ability," this ancient term passed through French and entered English as *faculty* and was in general use as early as 1490. The sense of "capacity to do something" is still preserved in the word by the fact that we say a fully competent person "has all his faculties."

With the rise of colleges and universities, deans and chancellors naturally sought adept and facile persons as teachers. As a result, a group of men fully competent to teach was known collectively as a faculty. The title indicated the whole body of masters and doctors with special ability in the four traditional departments of study: theology, law, medicine, and arts.

While some students of past and present may have doubted the power or ability of their professors, the venerable term of respect is still very much alive. In modern usage, any body of men and women engaged in teaching any subject to students of whatever age constitutes a *faculty*.

Commencement

According to present usage, it seems strange that *commencement* should be applied to the issuing of a diploma. *Finishment* would seem more logical.

But the word was entirely appropriate in early usage. For many years medieval universities required their graduates to spend a period teaching beginners. *Commencement*, therefore, did not mean that a man was released from an institution but that he ceased to be a pupil and commenced to teach.

Poser

Wealthy persons of Britain became interested in education many centuries ago. They established great universities such as Oxford and Cambridge, plus a host of preparatory schools, of which Eaton is the oldest. Many foundations were comparatively lax at first. But as timed passed, requirements became more and more strict.

By the sixteenth century, many schools had adopted the

practice of giving strict examinations. A special officer known as the apposer had the duty of opposing students—that is, framing hard questions to test them. Many a fellow must have performed this task effectively, for the examiner's title was clipped to *poser* and used to indicate any difficult question.

Alphabet

Educational materials were scarce, costly, and crude well into the sixteenth century. Textbooks of modern type were not yet in use. Teachers usually had a few books, while students seldom had more than a slate as long as they remained in the common schools that flourished in towns and villages.

In order to help beginning students learn their letters, the schoolmaster wrote them on his blackboard. Carefully arranged in orderly lines, such a pattern prepared as an example for pupils to copy was commonly known as a cross row.

Revival of interest in classical language and thought caused teachers to give special emphasis to Greek. In that tongue, *alpha* names the first character in the set of letters and *beta* stands for the second. Ancient Greeks used these two symbols to stand for the whole set of letters they used in writing, much as we say a child learns his ABC's.

Frequent use of the first two letters of the Greek system led to their being joined in popular speech, so that *alphabet* names any complete pattern ow written symbols, ancient or modern.

Academy

Among the civic attractions of Athens, Greece, was a beautiful suburban park. Complete with walks and fountains, it was a gift to the city from a wealthy citizen. Men of classical times gathered there much as those of later generations assemble in New York's Central Park and London's Trafalgar Square.

Socrates delivered some of his most noted orations in the Gardens of Academus. So it was natural that his pupil, Plato, should choose that place as a center for his own teaching. The philosopher established a school there in 387 B.C. and personally headed it for forty years. From the neighborhood in which it was located, Plato's institution came to be called the Academia. The effect of its widespread influence is felt today, for we still use *academy* to name institutions as diversified as a girl's boarding school and the West Point Military Academy.

To Burn the Midnight Oil

Fuel for lighting purposes has been an important factor in every stage of civilization. Both solid and liquid fuels were used in prehistoric times. Beeswax and tallow were the most important raw materials for candles, which became so expensive in the Middle Ages that they were seldom used except for ecclesiastical purposes.

Several types of vegetable and animal oils have been widely employed, and remained the staple source of illumination until recent times. Until the late eighteenth century, the typical lamp was a shallow vessel into which a short length of wick was dipped—to burn with much smoke and odor. Use of chimneys was launched late in that century, and fifty years later a Derbyshire gentleman began experimenting with the use of illuminating oil processed from petroleum-soaked shale.

It wasn't until 1859, however, that Edwin L. Drake's successful borings flooded the market with oil at low prices. Use of the new fuel from petroleum fostered importation of German-made lamps especially designed to burn it. Interest was so great that for twenty years the United States patent office received eighty applications a year for patents on lamps.

Development of cheap and abundant light led to a radical transition in the habits of college students. They began to stay up much later and often deferred their studies until the wee hours. Even in ancient times, it had been proverbial that a good student works late; now so many college boys were using new and inexpensive oil lamps to remain over their books long past the time respectable people went to bed that *to burn the midnight oil* came to indicate zeal in pursuit of learning.

Crisscross

Invention of the hornbook was a major landmark in education. Actually not a book at all, it was a sheet of vellum fastened to a board and covered with thin, translucent horn. Generations of children had no other device with which to learn their letters. It was in general use during the time of Shakespeare.

Pious makers of the hornbook usually printed the alphabet in large and small letters, followed by a benediction and the Lord's Prayer. Almost without exception, a bold cross was placed at the very beginning of the sheet as a tribute to the Savior.

Young scholars naturally tried to copy this Christ cross as well as the letters which followed it. Beginners often made the symbol quite clumsily, so by the late eighteenth century any pattern of crossed lines had come to be termed a *crisscross*.

Snob

The word comes from the Scottish *snab*, meaning "boy" or "servant." College students in England were at one time all members of the nobility—and applied *snab* in the sense of "servant" to the townsmen. The word *snab* was changed to *snob* in the 1600s when Cambridge University decided to admit commoners as students. Cambridge required that when registering, students describe their social position with the Latin words *Sine Nobilitate*, meaning "without nobility." The students abbreviated this to *S. Nob*. When spoken, this abbreviation seemed so much like the word *snab*, it came to be written *snob* and was used to signify a commoner who wished to mingle with the nobles.

XXIII

GEOGRAPHY AND WEATHER

Gotham □ **Iron Curtain** □ **Mumbo Jumbo** □
Calm □ **Dog Days** □ **Indian Summer** □

Gotham

A nursery rhyme, "The Merry Tales of the Mad Men of Gotham," published in the middle of the sixteenth century, describing a legendary village in England whose inhabitants were notorious for their foolishness, seems to be the recognized source of the name *Gotham*. It was applied to New York by Washington Irving in 1807 in the humorous periodical *Salmagundi,* which is also the name of a mixed dish of chopped meat and pickled herring with oil, vinegar, pepper, and onions, and therefore a potpourri. The word *Gotham* today, as we know it, means "a village or city where they have a mixed population."

Iron Curtain

The phrase was first used by Winston Churchill in a foreign affairs debate shortly after the Potsdam Conference in 1945. He described the difficulty of obtaining any reliable information about what was happening in Eastern Europe because of the *iron curtain,* which had divided the Continent. He used the phrase again a few months later in 1946 in his famous speech at Fulton, Missouri, when, with the president of the United States in the audience, he urged Anglo-American solidarity against the new danger arising from Soviet domination of Eastern Europe.

Mumbo Jumbo

Among the Kaffirs of Africa, polygamy was practiced until very recent times. In the case of wealthy men who had six or eight wives, quarrels between the women sometimes drove their spouses frantic.

Some distraught husband dreamed up a story about one Mumbo Jumbo, a mythical tribal ancestor who wore nothing but a mask and a tufted headdress. This demon, warned his inventor, would appear and chastise the women if they did not stop their squabbles.

They did not, so the cunning husband persuaded a friend to pose as the evil spirit. Coming to the house at dusk, he terrified all the wives, seized the chief offender, and gave her a thorough whipping. This stratagem became so effective that it was adopted as a tribal custom, its secret jealously guarded by the men.

As a result it became customary to speak of any meaningless ceremony intended to deceive the uninitiated as *mumbo jumbo*.

Calm

Many geographers believe that mild climate was responsible for the fact that Western civilization developed around the basin of the Mediterranean. Yet even in ancient Greece folk complained about the weather, adopting a special term for midday heat. They called the hottest part of a summer day *kauma*, from the word for "to burn."

Several months each year *kauma* affected the behavior of flocks. So the notion of stillness became attached to the name. Romans who adopted the Greek shepherd word pronounced it "calma." Little changed by centuries of use, the term designating the period when cattle lie still emerged into modern speech as *calm*.

Dog Days

Popular thought has always included breathless wonder at the meaning and role of heavenly bodies. Early Roman seers connected astronomical movements with many recurrent events on earth. One such relationship observed was the link between extreme summer heat and the rising of a prominent star. Since this body formed part of a dog-shaped constellation, Romans tagged it with their name for the animal and called it Canicula.

Modern scientists are uncertain whether the Romans were concerned with Sirius or with Procyon when they spoke of the star Canicula. But this much is clear: Before the first century of the Christian era, seers had decided that the rising of Canicula, its heat added to that of the sun, accounted for the most torrid portion of summer. So a period beginning in early July was called *dies caniculares* (days of the Dog Star).

Later observers of the heavens concluded, rightly, that the heat from Canicula has nothing to do with the oppressiveness of July. But the ancient term was so firmly fixed in popular speech that it has survived twenty centuries of change. Many superstitions concerning the prevalence of mad dogs during the *dog days* arose by association with the name of this period.

Indian Summer

Remnants of the racial tensions that existed between native Americans and the first wave of American immigrants still survive in our language today. One example might be "He who speaks with forked tongue." Another is the term *Indian summer*. The period of heat after summer has gone and before fall is over is, indeed, something of a false season—it promises us something that cannot be fulfilled. The American Indian in the time of America's budding development was greatly feared as suspicious and threatening. Like the pocket of warmth in October, Indians could not be counted on for long (to the white man's eye). And although Manhattan is now worth a little more than twenty-four dollars, we still refer to this last spell of warm weather as *Indian summer*.

SOURCES

Readers who wish to delve deeper into word lore will find it a fascinating hobby. However, practically all the major resources fall into the category of reference books, and many of them are out of print. Large libraries usually hold most of the titles listed below. These include not only word books themselves but also volumes useful in capturing the historical and social background underlying the development of a word or phrase.

In compiling and researching all the facts and material for this book I can truthfully say if it wasn't for the authors of the books listed below, the researchers and writers who did the earlier "digging," my job would have been very difficult.

Marvin Vanoni, 1988

Bartlett, John. *Familiar Quotations*. Boston, MA: Little, Brown & Co., 1948.

Bombaugh, C. C. *Facts and Fancies for the Curious*. Philadelphia, PA: J. B. Lippincott, 1905.

Dictionary of American History. New York, NY: Charles Scribner's Sons, 1940.

Dictionary of American Slang. New York, NY: The Macmillan Co., 1938.

Goldin, Hyman E. *Dictionary of American Underworld Lingo*. Boston, MA: Twayne Publishers, 1950.

McEwen, William A. *Encyclopedia of Nautical Knowledge*. Centerville, MD: Cornell Maritime Press, 1953.

Mathews, Mitford M. *Dictionary of Americanisms*. Chicago, IL: University of Chicago Press, 1951.

Menke, Frank G. *New Encyclopedia of Sports*. New York, NY: A. S. Barnes, 1947.

Morris, Richard B. *Encyclopedia of American History*. New York, NY: Harper & Bros., 1953.

Morris, W. & M. *Dictionary of Word and Phrase Origins*. New York, NY: Harper & Row Publishers, 1967.

Munn, Glenn G. *Encyclopedia of Banking and Finance*. Boston, MA: Bankers Publishing Co., 1949.

Oxford English Dictionary. New York, NY: Oxford University Press, 1888–1935.

Partridge, Eric. *Dictionary of Clichés*. New York, NY: The Macmillan Co., 1940.

Radford, Edwin & M. A. *Encyclopedia of Superstitions*. New York, NY: Philosophical Library, 1945.

Skeat, Walter W. *Concise Etymological Dictionary*. New York, NY: Clarendon Press, 1948.

Slonimsky, Nicolas. *Music Since 1900*. New York, NY: W. W. Norton & Co.,1938.

Stevenson, Burton. *Home Book of Quotations*. New York, NY: Dodd, Mead & Co., 1947.

Weekley, Ernest. *Concise Etymological Dictionary of Modern English*. New York, NY: E. P. Dutton, 1924.

Weseen, Maurice H. *Dictionary of American Slang*. New York, NY: Thomas Y. Crowell Co., 1934.

Wright, Joseph. *English Dialect Dictionary*. New York, NY: Oxford University Press, 1924.

———. *English Dialect Dictionary*. New York, NY: Oxford University Press, 1900.

———. *Romance of Names*. J. Murray, 1922.

———. *The Romance of Words*. New York, NY: E. P. Dutton, 1914.

———. *Surnames*. J. Murray, 1917.

INDEX